THE WORLD OF DYSLEXIA

*Understanding how to work
with the dyslexic brain.*

TABLE OF CONTENTS

INTRODUCTION

Congratulations on purchasing your copy of The World of Dyslexia: Understanding how to work with the dyslexic brain, and thank you for doing so.

The following chapters will discuss what dyslexia is, how it affects the individual, what we know about dyslexia, and what you can do to help, among other things.

There are plenty of books on this subject on the market, thanks again for choosing this one! Make sure to leave a short review on amazon if you enjoy it. I'd love to hear your thoughts. Every effort was made to ensure it is full of as much useful information as possible. Please enjoy!

Welcome to the World of Dyslexia

When someone you know suffers from dyslexia, it can be heart-wrenching to watch them struggle. There is nothing wrong with their intelligence, although sometimes it can seem that way not only to outsiders looking in, it can also feel that way to the one who is struggling to cope with the way their brain perceives the information it is receiving.

It is not a matter of there being something wrong with their eyes, either. It is a sort of disconnect or mismatch between what the eyes see and how the brain perceives it. It can almost feel like how some of us do when faced with an optical illusion. The problem is, this is not an illusion, even though the brain of someone with dyslexia may perceive it in such a way. For them, it is very real, and many people struggle with it every day. Their reality is distorted by the perception of their brains, and they have to slow down and adjust in order to understand what is "real" and not, with the illusions that their brains are feeding to them. Quite disconcerting indeed!

An individual struggling with dyslexia may even have difficulty reading simple words that they have seen multiple times over. They often need to slow their reading down and work hard to make sure that what their brain is processing is what they are actually seeing. Spaces between words may disappear, and words can blend together, seeming to make no sense at all. Words can flip around, not just backward, such as the word "now," turning into the word "won," but the letters can become jumbled and change the word "felt" into "left."

Writing and spelling can be just as challenging. Let's face it, language can be very difficult, even for someone to work small words out phonetically. "Of," phonetically, can easily be pronounced in the struggling mind of the dyslexic as "Uv."

When you have to work so hard just to understand the words on the paper, it can be very difficult to retain that information. Most of your brain's energy is being used up for the interpretation! The "win" becomes about making sense about something you are reading, or otherwise struggling through. The retention becomes lost in the translation, so to speak.

It becomes much easier for the retention of material to happen when it has another delivery method, such as sound... reading to someone with dyslexia, or letting them hear the information, versus seeing it, can be a much better way for them to retain what is being offered to them. They no longer have to struggle with the interpretation of what they are reading.

Sometimes this retention can cause difficulties in recalling words or remembering the right name for something they are trying to recall verbally as well. It is not that they don't know what it is, they just can't seem to recall the proper name for it. It becomes a nightmare of retention and recall that would drive the best of us to frustration!

Sadly, dyslexia can sometimes be difficult to diagnose, or if not in the right environment, the dyslexic can be left to struggle without any real clue that they could do far much better under different circumstances. It doesn't help that there are not only different levels of dyslexia, from mild to extreme, but not all dyslexics perceive things in the same way, or each may have different, or even just slightly different symptoms or perceptions. We are all unique!

The best thing we can do for the individual in our lives who has dyslexia is to utilize patience and understanding. So, let's move forward and learn what Dyslexia is first, so we can better understand how to work with it.

CHAPTER 1: WHAT IS DYSLEXIA?

The first published instance of developmental dyslexia was written in 1896 by Dr. W. Pringle Morgan of Sussex, England, for the British Medical Journal. He noted that despite the obvious intelligence and brightness of the subject, "Percy F," and that he was "quick at games, and in no way inferior to others of his age..." that he struggled with the ability to learn reading.

Dr. Morgan hit upon the initial recognition that there was a developmental issue that affected some extremely bright, intelligent people, and it directly related to their ability to learn and comprehend the written word. This was a dilemma that had confused scientists and researchers for centuries. They recognized the intelligence, but could not reconcile that with the individual's inability to learn reading at any level that came near to matching what was so obviously presented to them.

It has been discovered that 80-90% of those with learning disabilities have some form or level of dyslexia. Dyslexia itself affects over 20% of the population overall. It is far more common than we had normally thought until we took the time to begin learning about this developmental issue that affects so many!

In the past, and even yet today, there are those who struggle with dyslexia who go undiagnosed, even up to adulthood. Now, we are beginning to recognize the struggle of those who have dyslexia and are able to get them much needed help in their earlier years. The earlier that dyslexia can be diagnosed, the sooner we can get those who need our help, the care and attention that they need to thrive.

Those with dyslexia often have normal to above-average intelligence. They truly can succeed when given the right conditions under which to do so. Reading in any language can be difficult. It is a very complex process that we learn at an early age, wherein we connect sounds to the letters we see, and organized in the correct order, we can pull letters into words, words into sentences, and sentences into paragraphs. It is the very building blocks upon which our learning for the rest of our lives is based.

For someone with dyslexia, this is not so easy. The language processing areas of the brain are affected at varying levels, making it difficult, at best, for them to decode the letters and words and attach sounds to them. The letters become abstract things without sound. The combinations of letters get mixed up, so make no sense to the sounds that they are supposed to be connected to. With all of this going on, the basic building blocks of learning for someone with dyslexia are interrupted and jumbled, making moving forward in any direction with their learning a nightmare of trying to catch up and comprehend what is being taught to them.

For the dyslexic, there are neurological connections that are different than others. The wires in their brains are a bit jumbled, which is why the letters, words, and sounds become jumbled for them, unlike what the rest of us see and experience. Reading, writing, speaking, and spelling are all affected in varying degrees for someone who struggles with dyslexia. There is a connection that is missing that we need to help them find in a way that makes sense for them.

Causes of Dyslexia

The dyslexic brain, as we have touched upon briefly, is a neurological issue that creates difficulty in decoding words and sounds and matching them to what we know and perceive. This is not because those with dyslexia see words backward. They can be backward, jumbled, blurred, out of focus, or seen entirely different than what is written in its entirety.

Dyslexia has nothing whatsoever to do with the level of intelligence an individual does or does not have. It has been finally been discovered that there is a very strong genetic/hereditary link in those with dyslexia. They have even identified the genes that are connected to this issue, playing their own "role" so to speak, when it comes to the presence of dyslexia, but they have not yet discovered a cure or any way to "fix" it.

There is as high as a 50% likelihood that if a parent has dyslexia, that it will be passed on to their children. Regardless of any past assumptions that environmental factors during pregnancy, or in early childhood, are a cause for dyslexia, it has been discovered that this is not the case.

However, with work and persistence, since our brains can basically "rewire" themselves based on our own hard work and input, we can help those who struggle with dyslexia to overcome some of the problems that they face, and even learn and read more efficiently.

Attention Deficiency Hyperactivity Disorder (ADHD) has often been found to occur alongside dyslexia in individuals, but they are separate conditions, and having one does not necessarily mean that the other is present as well. It is interesting to note that the same portions of the brain that show more activity in those with ADHD, are similar in those with dyslexia. But they are separate and distinct conditions.

The neurological brain structure, and how the brain processes the written words or images taken in by someone struggling with dyslexia is different than those who do not. Those who have no trouble with reading, or interpreting the written word to having stronger input activity in the rear portion of the brain. Whereas those who struggle with dyslexia have stronger activity and processing through the front, left a portion of the brain.

The back of the brain is the area where science has shown us words are formed. This part of the brain becomes highly active when people who are strong readers are soaring through written paragraphs and pages. It is like accessing an instant databank of words, ready to wait, at their disposal.

Those with dyslexia struggle with the left, frontal portion of the brain. It does not mean that they cannot read; it just takes them longer and is not nearly as effective or efficient. Many eventually learn to compensate for some of the left brain reading by using the front, right portion of the brain. This can help them overall with comprehension, and they do become more accurate readers in this way, but their efforts are still slow and painstaking. It is this inefficient pattern of brain activity and is one of the main root causes of dyslexia.

It still has yet to be discovered the *why* of why a dyslexic's brain processes through an area different than the rest of us. Science doesn't even fully understand why the different areas of the brain process things in different ways yet. There is no one, single area that is specifically utilized and dedicated to the reading process overall, and they are still trying to sort through exactly how our brains work the way they do for something so seemingly simple in our learning process.

Science has not been able to discover as of yet what the underlying cause of dyslexia is, but some discoveries have been made to help us move in the right direction. The left, front portions of the brain that register more activity when those with dyslexia try to read have difficulty, at best, when trying to process how language "sounds." When trying to break apart these basic sounds, also called phonemes (FO-neems), those sounds become jumbled in the brain of the dyslexic and are difficult for them to break apart into smaller portions. Science has come to call this the phonological processing impairment theory, which adequately describes the difficulty facing those who struggle with dyslexia.

What have we been able to determine as to the cause of dyslexia? It has already been determined that while there is a higher probability of having dyslexia if you are born into a family where it is already present. However, heredity has been ruled out as an actual cause. So, where do we look next?

Some are searching to find the answers in genetics. There is the hope, that if a gene can be isolated and determined to cause dyslexia, then there is the possibility that help may be found for some dyslexic sufferers in the creation of targeted gene therapy.

In the UK, there is a non-profit organization dedicated to learning disability, called the Dyslexia Research Trust. Their studies have implicated two chromosomes so far, 6 and 18, in their research of dyslexia development. One of these particular genes, KIAA0319, has demonstrated a direct correlation with low-performance results in tests involving spelling, reading, phonology, and orthography. Independent research has made the same connection as the Dyslexia Research

Trust with the involvement of this gene in those with dyslexia.

We are still a long way away from gene therapy involving this chromosome, but at least we may have found a beginning. It takes time to determine exactly what the gene is, what it does, how it impacts the individual, and how it is either activated or repressed.

It has also been determined, unlike was thought even a short time ago, that any manner of environmental factors is a consideration. This is not something that happens because of a mother's exposure to drugs, smoking, alcohol, contact with heavy metals, or any other chemicals during pregnancy. It also is not due to any lack of vitamins or minerals during pregnancy, either.

There have been cases of such things as heavy metal or toxin exposures for toddlers where their symptoms have presented like dyslexia, but once given the proper care and treatment, those symptoms have disappeared, indicating that it was not dyslexia at all, as long as these symptoms are caught while the child is still very young.

Another form of dyslexia noted as "Acquired Dyslexia," has been found in cases of those suffering from a form of dyslexia following a trauma such as a stroke, but it isn't dyslexia in the traditional sense of the definition. It only presents in the same way. Sometimes it does involve damaged portions of the brain that once acted like everyone else's, lighting up in the rear portions, but damage to those sensitive areas have forced the brain to remap itself and utilize different portions, such as the front left part of the brain that lights up in the cases of those born with dyslexia.

The simplified explanation of the cause of dyslexia comes down to it being genetic, and in part, hereditary. The brain of someone with dyslexia processes language in a different way than someone who does not have this condition.

Diagnosing Dyslexia

Dyslexia is not specifically listed under the Americans with Disabilities Act (ADA), although it is considered a learning disability that can highly impact and limit major life activities, which include learning and learning. In this case, those with dyslexia are protected from discrimination. However, there has yet to be formed any federal law that defines exactly how individuals should be tested for dyslexia to arrive at a diagnosis.

Guidance and advice for how to proceed to such a determination and diagnosis are provided by the National Center for Learning Disabilities (NCLD). They have stated:

"Professionals with expertise in several fields are best qualified to make a diagnosis of dyslexia. The testing may be done by a single individual or by a team of specialists. A knowledge and background in psychology, reading, language and education are necessary. The tester must have a thorough working knowledge of how individuals learn to read and why some people have trouble learning to read. They must also understand how to administer and interpret evaluation data and how to plan appropriate reading interventions."

So, how do they decide then, as to whether or not an individual is dyslexic, and whether or not they are affected to the extent that it is considered a disability? The International Dyslexia Association has composed a list of things for consideration. These include:

- Background Information
- Speaking and Listening Abilities (Oral Language Abilities)
- Spelling
- Word Reading and Recognition
- Phonological Processing
- Decoding Skills
- Text Reading and Comprehension
- Vocabulary
- Fluency

They further provide a framework for the testing evaluation detailing both weaknesses and strengths in each of these areas. It is stated that the testing should be done by a familiar professional, specifically with dyslexia and/or other forms of language and literacy disorders. They also suggest that the entire process is not just about the testing scores themselves, but that there are definitive eligibility cut-off points, although there is an awareness that states themselves provide some of these cut-off scores, and can vary from state to state. Included in the reports should be recommendations to plan for intervention.

Some signs can be watched for that may help to determine the potential of someone having dyslexia, which can then lead to further testing. These are traits often commonly found in those who have already been diagnosed with dyslexia. Since dyslexia presents in different ways with different individuals, not everyone is going to exhibit the same symptoms or signs in the same way, but it can be a general rule of thumb that if someone you know is commonly experiencing at least ten of the points listed below, it may be worth considering to have them tested for the presence of dyslexia.

- An individual that has been called dumb, lazy, careless, or immature, accused of having behavioral troubles or that they are not trying hard enough.

- Someone who may otherwise seem intelligent, bright, and articulate, but has difficulties in writing, reading, or spelling at their grade level.

- An individual who may show to have a high IQ, but has difficulties academically and can pass oral exams better than written ones.

- Someone who has low self-esteem and may feel dumb, but can compensate well to cover up or hide any weaknesses. When it comes to school testing or reading, they may become emotional or easily frustrated.

- An individual who may tend to daydream a lot, or zone out, maybe losing track of time regularly basis. Perhaps they have a low attention span and or sometimes be a little hyperactive.

- Someone who learns better when presented with hands-on experiences, visual aids, demonstrations, or through observation.

- An individual who may get stomach aches, dizziness, or headaches when trying to read.

- Someone who can become confused with letters and numbers, or sequences of words or numbers.

- An individual whose reading, or especially writing, displays repeated words or symbols (numbers), extras, letter and/or numbers transposed or left out or substituted, or sometimes even reversed.

- Someone who may say that the letters and/or numbers move around when they are trying to read.
- An individual who complains of vision problems yet seems fine during an eye exam.
- Someone who may have to read and re-read things, and still may have difficulty comprehending what they have read.
- An individual who is inconsistent with their ability to spell, and may write things down phonetically ("uv" instead of "of").
- Someone who may seem to get distracted by sounds, or may seem to hear things differently than what is actually said.
- An individual who has trouble forming words or thoughts leaves sentences or thoughts incomplete, has trouble when pronouncing long words, or mixes up words with multiple syllables or longer phrases.
- Someone who may have illegible handwriting has difficulties when copying or writing, and may have an unusual grip on their writing implement.
- An individual who may suffer from motion sickness, or has difficulty when performing tasks that involve fine, and sometimes even gross motor skills.
- Someone who may show signs of being ambidextrous, and can sometimes confuse left from right, or under from over.

- An individual who may be consistently late struggles with telling or managing time or has difficulties remembering the steps in a sequential task.

- Someone who can adequately find the answers to mathematical problems, but can't always demonstrate it on paper, or may do a lot of "finger counting" when working out mathematical problems.

- An individual who struggles with counting the number of objects, or dealing with money, even though they demonstrate that they do know how to count.

- Someone who has no real troubles with arithmetic, but struggles with word problems and higher forms of math, such as algebra.

- An individual with excellent long-term memory skills, especially when involving faces, experiences, or locations.

- Someone who has difficulty remembering sequences, or retaining facts or information for things and places that they have not experienced themselves.

- An individual whose internal dialogue involves more feelings or images as opposed to words or sounds.

- Someone who can be either compulsive with the need for order, or can be extremely disordered.

- An individual who can be one of several things... extremely quiet, a troublemaker, or even the class clown.
- Someone who may be prone to food sensitivities, chemicals, or other additives, or may have a lot of ear infections.
- An individual who may have developed a little later than most as defined by developmental stages such as crawling, walking, talking, or even tying their shoes.
- Someone who may have been a late bedwetter, or maybe an extra light or heavy sleeper.
- An individual may exhibit high or low pain tolerances.
- Someone who may be either emotionally sensitive has a strong sense of justice or continually strives for perfection.
- An individual whose symptoms or mistakes increase when they feel pressured by time, poor health, emotional stress, or they become confused.

Adults can often present differently than children when it comes to dyslexia because they have had years of learning how to cope with and even hide some of the frustrations and difficulties that they face. The bottom line is, even as an adult, dyslexia can be diagnosed, and steps can be taken to help aid their ability to cope with how their brain processes things in their lives, especially when connected with reading and writing. We will be covering some of these techniques in later chapters within this book.

The Prognosis for Those with Dyslexia

The prognosis for most who have dyslexia is actually good. It is hard to define a specific prognosis, because of the range of how dyslexia affects individuals, and to what extent it affects them. The severity levels differ from individual to individual. However, as was said previously, the earlier a diagnosis is made, the better the chances for those who have dyslexia to develop coping methods for dealing with this disability.

One of the most important things to learn is that dyslexia has nothing to do with levels of motivation or intelligence. It also has nothing to do with bad parenting or laziness. Dyslexia can be helped with simple accommodations made in reading interventions, and through support, praise, and other forms of encouragement.

Those who have milder forms of dyslexia are going to have an easier time finding ways to overcome their struggles. This is the same for those who have supportive circles in family, friends, teachers, and co-workers. Even those who have a tougher road ahead of them due to a lack of these things, or due to having a more severe form of dyslexia, even though dyslexia is not something that can be outgrown, or just goes away, with work and dedication, they can still go to college or work toward success in life pursuits.

Part of their ability to do so lies in the ability of the brain to retrain itself. The plasticity of the way the brain maps the neural pathways allows for reversing and repairing pathways to lead toward a stronger ability to not only read but comprehend that which is being read.

While plasticity is something that is considered to be a stronger trait of a younger mind, certain reading programs that have been developed to help rewire the brain have proven to be highly effective in adults as well. It allows the brain to create new pathways to compensate for how the dyslexic mind processes things. It still is, of course, easier to accomplish when done at a younger age, but it also offers hope for those who are only now being diagnosed with dyslexia, even as adults.

CHAPTER 2: ABOUT DYSLEXIA
THE PSYCHOLOGICAL DISTRESS
OF DYSLEXIA

When we are speaking on the terms of learning, we tend to break down learning into two concepts, intelligence, and interpretation. Dyslexia affects interpretation, whereas it does not have anything to do with general intelligence. Those who consider individuals who have dyslexia to be less intelligent may not be seeing the entire picture. In fact, it is beginning to be found, that those whose brains handle language and words phonetically, as well as in what order those words logically belong, have very high intelligence.

The brain, when very active, tends to formulate everything in the style of memory. Our brain's memory is not in any way, similar to the written word. Considering that we are using words to teach and learn, we must also take into mind that all brains remember everything in a very disunited order. Almost relating to fragments. Education is not conducted in fragments.

Dyslexia is a term used to describe a disorder that involves difficulty in learning. This learning extends to reading, interpreting words, letters, and other symbols. The term 'difficulty' is also a concept that needs examination. Learning is already a stressful, imposing, and all-around demanding discipline. There may be many outside influences that cause loss of learning.

Difficulty with any skill takes time. The difficulty in learning is no different than any other skill. Some take to skills easier than others. The difficulty lies not in the individual trying to learn but in the difficulty of learning itself.

To better understand the psychological distress related to dyslexia, we can look at the different forms of it. Typically, there are five to seven forms of dyslexia. We can break down each one and then get a better understanding of what the human mind does when it is under the stress of learning in these situations. The five forms of dyslexia we are going to examine are:

- Phonological Dyslexia
- Surface Dyslexia

- Rapid Naming Deficit
- Double Deficit Dyslexia
- Visual Dyslexia

When we think of dyslexia, we may be inclined to think of the transposition of letters. In fact, the human mind is a very complex organ and can take transposition as a form of higher functioning. To play with letters and symbols is already hardwired into our nature. The mind is naturally comfortable with fragments.

Consider the first form of dyslexia on our list, phonological. Phonological dyslexia is directly related to the sounds of language versus the writing of that language. It is the similarities of the human speech that is the issue here. The basic sounds of language, especially English, are not distinct.

Amongst the over 170,000 English words that currently are in use, multiple words have similar sounds within them. Simply spoken, many words sound the same.

With that many words in use, and the fact there are so few letters in our alphabet, there is no question that we all hear words differently when we hear them spoken. Not only that, consider the number of accents and forms of the English spoken word. Meaning, as well as slang, combined with a rural accent, and pronunciation can make English insanely complex.

Then we are going to write it down. Often this is not as the word sounds.

Nevertheless, a consideration that there are also about 6,500 unique languages spoken all over the globe can contest written word against spoken word. In other words, we write things down.

Language has an immense complexity. There are many examples where writing and speaking, not always being the same phonetically. Those who are working with dyslexia take this one step further. Two words that sound the same can be switched in the mind. It is only logical to find a solution that translates sound into writing. When that sound does not match the written word, it is only understandable that the human mind rejects the confusing.

Let us work with the words: prescribe and describe. They sound almost exactly the same. An active mind will work with those sounds. In fact, that active mind may transpose the written words with each other because they sound alike. There is nothing to say that these two similar-sounding words can have similar definitions when written down on the page. So why not use each word for each other's definition or each other for that matter. They sound the same, right?

So, now prescribe is the same word used to describe. Please describe the medication. This is the emotional stress of phonological dyslexia. Getting our actual message incorrect on something as important as medication.

When basic sounds get transposed in our minds, the written word may get transposed as well. Looking at basic sound may be taken to the extreme. The written word often does not sound like the spoken word. Take the word knife for an example. Why the k silent? We do not pronounce, "I need a knife for my butter, please." We say, please pass me that knife so I can spread my butter, please".

This example is not the direct definition of phonological dyslexia. However, the silent k is a fact that the written word does not always represent the spoken word. This incongruity is not logical. For those who already stress over linguistics, sound needs to be written as it sounds. It is not logical to have a rule in a language where a word is spelled differently than how everyone, and we mean everyone, pronounces it. Get rid of that rule.

Logic equates to intelligence. Intelligence tells us that the sound of words is not always what is written on the page, so to follow the rules of writing, is not logical. When there is no logic to a structure, learning the written word is illogical.

Consider how much we speak to each other. Also, consider how much we listen to each other. Then compare listening skills to reading skills. How much do we really read in our lifetimes? Do we come from the spoken word or the written word?

These two questions are easily answered. We communicated by a speech before we ever communicated by the written word.

It is only natural to accept that the written word is not as powerful as the spoken word. So, why do we attach so much attention to it? An accurate translation of our spoken word looks incredibly messy on the page. Phonological dyslexia understands that speaking came first. So, why not work words around so that they are like they are when spoken? It is illogical to not try to fix the written word so that it sounds like the spoken word. So, the mind does it for them.

This is slow stress that requires an immense amount of concentration on behalf of the individual who has dyslexia and the person with whom they are trying to communicate.

Similar sounds being transposed in the written word, with two words that sound similar, are the defining psychological difficulty of phonological dyslexia.

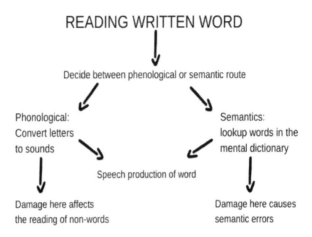

READING WRITTEN WORD

Decide between phenological or semantic route

Phonological:
Convert letters
to sounds

Semantics:
lookup words in the
mental dictionary

Speech production of word

Damage here affects
the reading of non-words

Damage here causes
semantic errors

Let us take a look at surface dyslexia.

The psychological distress of this form of dyslexia is a more physical experience. Surface dyslexia most often occurs with individuals who have experienced trauma to their brains from some outside physical damage.

Surface dyslexia is the mind of seeing one form of the word as its definitive meaning.

Surface dyslexia is a simplified version of a complex system. A word that is spelled like another word needs to sound like that word when we speak it. Otherwise, our brains keep one word and reject the other. When we are working with surface dyslexia, we are looking at the pronunciation of words and what order we give them.

Let us use an example so that we can understand what we are dealing with. Take two words again. Mint and pint. They do not really sound the same when spoken; however, they are spelled similarly. When the human mind learns that mint is pronounced mint and pint is pronounced pint, then pint is rejected because why would we have two words that are spelled the same that are not pronounced the same?

The outright rejection of the mind to even see a word is immensely distressing. We are talking about questioning sanity here. Trust in that; if you are someone who deals with this, this is not about sanity. It may feel like you are insane, and that your mind is out of control, however, there are reasons why the experience is so disorienting.

Surface dyslexia wants the brain to read and write words about how they are pronounced. Consider that there are two ways to read English words. These two ways are referred to as pathways, and those pathways are lexical or word-based.

Lexical direct and indirect are the two ways we read. The direct pathway is knowing that a word is written is not always the way it is pronounced. The indirect pathway is sounding out of the word into pronunciation.

Those that are working with surface dyslexia tend to pronounce their way through any written word. This is the preservation of the indirect method of reading. In the majority of cases, it is the best way to read.

Have you ever been told to just sound out a word so that you can spell it? This is the default for our brains. As for our two words... mint and pint. Mint has the sound "in," in the word. Pint has a sound of "ien" in its word. If the word pint is spelled "pient," then keep it. If a pint is really spelled pint then we already have mint, so reject it.

We do not wish to contradict direct and indirect lexical pathways; however, it seems they are logically reversed. There is no logical sense to have rules that make it so that words are *not* pronounced like they are spelled. Removing the double negative, saying, and spelling is the same. Yet, the "direct" pathways are not logical or simple. They direct pathways to obey rules that are illogical when dealing with pronunciation.

Simply speaking, we are taught letters in a specific order. So, why not follow that order when we are working with the written word? Why do we not speak the same letters the same ways for each word?

This is the translucency of a language. English is very translucent versus opaque. This means that there are many English words that break pronunciation rules making the language transparent. Words are spoken differently from the written word in a way that is very illogical. Rule-breaking with pronunciation is the transparency of a language.

What we are trying to discern is how the rules of the English language work and why they are so stressful.

A human mind, either physically damaged or not, has to work with the illogical formulas of the written word to achieve excellence in education. Eventually, we need to conclude that education needs to be based on something other than the written word. Maybe someone will give an individual with dyslexia the ability to come up with something new for education.

Check out what happens to dyslexia as a diagnosis when we logically remove the written word from our education system.

When we hypothetically say that the written word is no longer the guidance stick of education, dyslexia is no longer. Period. All dyslexia goes away. In other words, if you are diagnosed with dyslexia, there is great stress placed upon you to conform to education. Maybe it is the education that needs to conform to you.

Back to surface dyslexia. When we are not just transposing words, and we are eliminating words because they do not fit logic or pronunciation, we are now questioning more than just a learning disorder. We are looking to our minds as to what level of sanity we have.

The question often asked by those diagnosed with dyslexia is, why does my brain work so differently from everyone else? Am I truly deficient?

Surface dyslexia can be immensely distressing due to the minds' pure rejection of words. There is a saying that those who are truly insane do not know it. This is something to consider when dealing with surface dyslexia. When the mind rejects automatically without consent, this is extremely frightening.

And those with surface dyslexia know their brains are rejecting words. A word that is not pronounced as it is spelled is ejected. That is terrifying.

Those who are suffering a mind that rejects words completely know that their minds are rejecting words completely. This is not insanity; in fact, it is logical. When you already have an M in place for mint, why do we really need a P to only change that word to something that sounds nothing like the original word mint? The rejection of that word is logical.

A single rule exists.

What we say and how we sound it out is what we write.

For if something does not play by the rules, and in this, we mean the basic rule of writing as we speak, reject that word, and get it out of here.

The written word is very complex indeed and has a whole bunch of rules.

Rapid Naming Deficit

Not all those with dyslexia have issues with rapidly naming things. Letters, numbers, and colors may be very difficult to process when presented to an individual, with or without dyslexia. Eventually, those dealing with the rapid naming deficit, get to the name of the objects they see. It is the speed of the processing of the mind that is being measured here.

Fast, accelerated, slow, stinted are all words associated with the speed of education. The same applies to read. The same applies to the recognition of any object or series of objects in this world.

First off, considering speed when we equate intelligence is manically stressful. Those who are already having to concentrate on the word being the word have to go slower when presented with a series of words.

Unfortunately, in English society, speed is something we have put a great value on.

To those who require a bit of processing time inside their minds to determine if that color on the wall is orange or purple, or if it is spelled the way it is, speed equates eventually to pressure. Nevertheless, to process a series of colors in a sharp flashing speed is stressful for someone who is struggling.

There is eventually a downfall and possibly mental psychological scarring that takes place when an individual cannot keep up with the required speed. This damage can even lead to an eventual transposition of concept to a word.

Some can say that the classroom is set up to teach as many children as possible as quickly as possible. This can imprint mistaken concept to word in a permanent fashion. For example.

At a very young age, we are taught what colors are.

Is this color red or blue? Blue.

Now we are going to teach that child to learn colors as fast as they can.

Red, blue, red, red, orange, green, red, blue... Red? Is orange really spelled like that? No blue, no, wait... red.

And now green is red. Why? Because the pressure on the mind made it so. Because of the speed of knowing your colors is essential in a classroom. Because we are graded on how fast we can be tested.

Nevertheless, something serious happens when the mind is allowed to examine color. The logical, intelligent mind will go through all colors before it assigns any color. This means that if a student is in a rush or under pressure, blue becomes red, and red becomes blue. No, wait, that red is green.

Speed is everything when we consider the learning capacity of the human mind. Unfortunately for us, the written word is all about speed. What do we mean by that?

For a child to pick up a book about colors and read it, is about speed. A super-intelligent child will examine every color with every other color in a slow, methodical way. Outside pressures say read as fast as everyone else. Speed may be the cause of transposition and confusion. Who is honestly to say that a child who examines every color in a logical way by comparing it to all other colors, is incorrect or "slow"?

This is not to say this the only solution to a complex issue like rapid naming deficit being speed. Well, rapid being a word in the explanation itself makes it a speed issue. Rapid is the existence of speed.

This speed is very traumatic to those who want to examine every word on the page so that they get that word correct.

Recall of word in a rapid way is also traumatic. They say intelligence is the ability to find all solutions and then simplify.

That takes time. For those diagnosed with the rapid naming deficit, consider that speed does not equate to intelligence.

When they take their time, find all solutions, then simplify, they may be the ones to teach a new form of speed.

Being allowed to take time is the pressure we all feel. Speed may be our psychological downfall, whether we are diagnosed dyslexia or not. We must take a look at the fact that we are more complex than one-dimensional beings on a stopwatch.

Double deficit dyslexia, is the combination of more than one form of dyslexia.

The double deficit is not always just double. Triple and even a conglomerate of dyslexic conditions may stem from an individual struggling to make the mind work. There is also the fact that dyslexia is still a continuously rediscovered condition. What we mean by this is that there is no real way to measure the complexities and combinations of mind. When we consider how the mind functions, we eventually come to the conclusion that we are just beginning to explore our mental abilities.

When we are looking at a double deficit in an individual, we are working with a multidirectional issue. This is to say that we may experience various mild versions of phonetic conversion to word and various major inabilities to rapidly repeat subjects, symbols, or words.

This is not to say that there are no specifics within double deficit dyslexia. There are very specific combinations. However, since the human mind is so complex, there are going to be crossovers from one diagnosis to another.

This can add additional stress to someone who is diagnosed with a double deficit. When it is difficult to pinpoint what conditions with which we are working, we are in a state of confusion. In addition, we are now looking at more than one condition. When we see that we have something we need or want to work on, and then someone stacks multiple jobs on us, we stress.

Then when we take into account it is our own minds coming up with new ways to handle language, we stress more.

There is no doubt that a human mind that decides to play with words or sounds one way will just ignore the other ways it can play. Those who have had physical damage to their brains will find that the human mind compensates by changing its entire system. Similarities become an easier way to live, and the mind falls into a pattern for how to process all data. To call that deficient may be an insult to simplicity.

One can say that it is unfair to anyone, to say they are doubly deficient.

This applies to anything in life. It is a language that we mostly are working with when dealing with dyslexia. Calling someone doubly deficient is not a kind or gentle way to describe anything with language.

So, since we are talking here about the psychological side effects of dyslexia, we might as well talk about language. The language used to deal with those who struggle with language is currently extremely harsh. Since the labels, we put on those who are suffering and struggling come from those who have had immense schooling, their use of language is not the same as those who are diagnosed. Turning to those who are diagnosing dyslexia, to use more gentle language, is not out of reach, considering it is the language they are examining.

Ask those who are living with dyslexia what they think double deficit means. There is a doubt that they will look upon it kindly. In fact, it may cause some psychological-emotional damage.

Relief comes from accepting who and what we are. When we have more than one "type" of dyslexia, we merely need to break it down and work on life, bit by bit.

Let us say someone is struggling with colors and how to spell them. Blue. This is not blue. This word is spelled Blu. And in turn, when blue gets confused with turquoise and vice versa, this individual goes directly to double deficit. Why? Because they have used the mind to logically go from pronunciation to rejection?

The point here is that it may be too easy to put someone with dyslexia into this double category. Consider the word blue again.

Blu leads to turquoise or Blu, sometimes they are the same or exchanged.

This leads to blue not being recognized at all.

This combination of phonological surface and rapid can most definitely occur. It is up to us to make it so that those who are actually experiencing these difficulties to be gentle with our language to describe the condition.

In more ways than one, the word deficit needs to be removed from the equation.

There are other forms of dyslexia that we are finding every day. For example, visual dyslexia is a new form of surface dyslexia. It is a more specific term used to describe the look of a word.

Unfortunately, there are many new styles or forms of dyslexia that is not entirely based on enough research. In the condition of visual dyslexia, there is the bottom line of fact that we are looking at the mind, not in the eyes.

The way we visually perceive life is not the same as how we process information or symbol or word. Vision is only partially mental, and only by connection. To say a mental issue is visual is stretching limits. Vision is not the same as touch.

Yet both are connected, the eyes do feel when hitting with intense light. It is unfair to call someone suffering from learning, visually impaired because they see things differently.

We are talking about the language here. Let us be careful and specific with our use of it.

So, the bottom line is that we get distressed when our minds do not work like everyone else. Distress itself is a psychological, logical, emotional, and often physical condition. So now we may want to ask, what is the psychological distress associated with dyslexia?

First off, let us take into consideration what psychological distress is. Taking a very complex concept and simplifying it is the best way to define something.

Psychological Distress Is Not Feeling Well

It so happens that psychological anything is a mental scientific examination of how the mind works. Psychological distress happens in and with our emotions.

Dyslexic individuals normally have full awareness that their minds are rebelling. This is not a comfortable feeling. In fact, there are many negative emotions that are directly attached to dyslexia. These negative emotions often get in the way of improving dyslexia. It is, indeed, psychological distress.

Anger

Anger is often the most direct emotion that is attached to dyslexia. Anger that you are not working well, or fast enough. Anger that you cannot do what everyone else does. Anger that you are unable to understand something that everyone else understands. Anger that you are different.

All of the reasons for the anger listed above are valid and justified. Well, some may be judged; however, most are factually based and justified. Let us take a moment and look at what emotions are and how they are related to dyslexia. Then we can look at what we can do to help a bit with these emotions.

The human mind tends to lean to one side more than the other. When we take apart the mind and look at each side, we begin to see that there are two basic philosophies for what we are. We think logically. We think emotionally. The mind is already split in two for a reason. That reason is the balance between logic and emotion.

When the human mind rejects logic, it becomes very emotional. This is because emotions are in us to take over when we are overloaded logically.

Consider fear. When we get to a place where our lives are in danger, and we do not know what to do anymore, we stop being logical and become emotional. Fear is information for us to take action. That may be standing really still. It may be to fight back. The situation is the condition of what action to take. Fear happens when logic fails.

With the case of dyslexia, we are looking at a very logical mind, not functioning normally in a relatively safe environment. These minds that are mostly logical have their logic fail and must fall back on emotion.

First off, let us begin by saying that those with dyslexia are not emotionally stunted. All we are saying is that dyslexia tends to mess about with the logic of learning. When logic fails, what we have left is emotion.

This is why dyslexia is supremely psychologically distressful.

When logic fails, our emotions take over and get loud. What we mean by loud is that our inner voices begin to scream uncontrollably. This is not unlike what anger is. Loss of control is often found in anger. The inability to stay in the moment is anger. Not understanding and losing control happens when we are angry.

These are all emotionally created events from the frustration of logic failing us when we try to read, and the letters jump around.

So, what do we do with these emotions? Do we just let them run rampant through our reading and cause chaos? Well, the anger attached to dyslexia is mostly justified. Unfortunately, to those who pressure others to be successful readers, distance is key.

Yes, when reading makes you angry, do not read so much. This is not to say stop reading completely. This is to say if your mind is getting in the way of your reading and education, and you're feeling angry, maybe your mind needs to be curbed for a while.

This needs to be done safely. The escaping from the mind or the putting of the mind on hold can be very dangerous. Many have tried to slow down their minds with various chemicals or exercises. We do not really condone the use of any drug to slow our minds. We also do not recommend constant escaping into unreal worlds.

So, how do you avoid the mind and still work on reading?

With the intelligence, of course.

Intelligence is improved not by doing the same thing over and over, but by doing many things. What is meant by this is that someone who suffers reading disorders may want to consider that there are more ways to increase intelligence than just reading.

Consider intelligence for a moment. First off, it is difficult to define intelligence and education in the same breath. Education has a measuring ruler that has little to do with intelligence; education is about diligence.

And if you are dyslexic, you may find difficulties between intelligence and diligence. Those two words look a lot alike, don't they?

Let us be perfectly clear; they are not the same.

Education is about diligence. Success in education is mostly about the ability to stick it out and get to the end.

Read and keep reading and keep reading until your anger consumes you to a place of despair and sadness, will not accomplish diligence. This is not to say that all students are unhappy. There is great pride in the success of diligence.

We are under a timeline here. Education needs to happen at a specific time. This means pressure to remain in a place of reading over and over again until the person who has dyslexia completes education and graduates with their friends, is the goal.

Take a moment to consider that, under the conditions of education, anger is telling us something. We get angry, not because we are meant to be in a place of non-control. We get angry because logic fails, and emotion is trying to tell us to do something else to get around what is in our way.

Intelligence is something that can be trained alongside education as a reminder to the mind that it is not really failing; it is just struggling with a specific skill. The best thing to do when you struggle with a skill is to bookmark it and go work on something else for a while. When we raise other skills around the skill with which we struggle, that skill improves without us having to concentrate on it so much.

When you struggle with dyslexia, there are seven other types of intelligence you can work on until your anger subsides.

Before we list all seven, some of the greatest minds of our time (Albert Einstein, for example) have stated plainly that intelligence is only raised by utilizing multiple intelligences and not just specializing in one.

So, all seven it is then.

- Linguistic. (writing, reading)
- Logical-Mathematical (patterns, categories, relationships)
- Bodily-Kinesthetic (knowledge through bodily sensations)
- Spatial (images and pictures in space)
- Musical (instruments including the human instrument)
- Interpersonal (communication with others)
- Intrapersonal (aware of own feelings)

Notice how the first one always listed is Linguistic. That is most likely because the current education system is based on it. And we relate education to intelligence.

For those who are angry that their brains reject linguistic skills, take a look at all those other skills that can be worked on to improve intelligence. There is nothing to say that the current system in that those affected by dyslexia need to focus on just one form of intelligence. There is hope, even in education, that music and the will to understand it is necessary to raise intelligence.

When anger takes over, maybe there is a need to improve intelligence by means of say, spatial intelligence. The beauty in this system is that when we raise the general intelligence of an individual, they become so much more able to pick up a new skill quickly. More intelligence equates to better learning skills down the road.

It is up to the person who is suffering in anger of dyslexia to stand up and take on another form of intelligence. They can come back to linguistics. Give them a break and maybe even some praise for attempting another form of intelligence.

This will allow for action to replace anger. Less anger equals the ability to work on the intelligence form that is the most difficult for whoever is trying to improve themselves. In the case of dyslexia, we are trying to remove anger by replacing it with improved alternative intelligence.

If you are reading this and you are diagnosed with dyslexia, understand that language is only one-seventh of the recognized intelligence forms. Honestly, who is to say that someone who cannot do one of seven intelligences, has a 'deficit.'

Can your diagnosing doctor do all seven equally? Maybe, and maybe not.

Yes, this book is about making things easier for the dyslexic dealing with the linguistic form of the seven intelligences. This chapter is about how to handle the psychological distress of not being able to do linguistics well. A fact we often overlook is, linguistics is only a small part of being intelligent. So, maybe not the end of the world if we are better at music than linguistics.

So, when you have dyslexia, or you are helping someone who has dyslexia, please try to keep an objective mind and realize that there are six complete other ways to raise intelligence. Maybe that may help everyone involved to not be so angry about not being able to do a skill.

Mostly what we have to work with when we are using medical science to define dyslexia is research.

Research on the subject of dyslexia is mostly working with children. In addition to that, research on the mind is in its infancy. Research for dyslexia is not to be discouraged, because the more information we have, the more we are knowledgeable about any subject.

As of now, most research is about children.

When we talk about research, we may want to consider that dyslexia was first diagnosed over a hundred years ago. Current research is telling us the same facts.

There is always going to be a child who is very intelligent and has difficulty reading. Almost every teacher has such a student.

Without going into a ton of medical detail, basic research says three things about those with dyslexia.

One is that there is an area of the brain that is related to language. Some brains are just not born with that section developed to the standard of everyone else. The left parietotemporal system and the left occipitotemporal area are two parts of the brain that are linked with reading and language.

Some brains are not developed as much as others in this location. Some brains have been damaged and have difficulty accessing this section of the brain. Being different does not necessarily equate to deficient.

Look, all brains, as in all humans, are a bit different. It is ok to be different. When we are all the same, something happens to our freedoms. So, let us all be different and help each other with whatever part of our brains are struggling, with each of the intelligences.

Second is that research has shown that when we image a brain with dyslexia, we find that more activity takes place in other areas. This is to say that when an individual has to say lost sight, other senses improve to take the place of sight. Normally those who are blind tend to hear much better than those with sight.

Most likely, those who are diagnosed with dyslexia have brain imaging that shows more activity in other areas, and that means they may be more adept with skills other than reading.

Finally, research tells us that there is no cure for dyslexia. As of now, there is no way to go into the brain and develop a section like the left parietotemporal system.

Maybe someday, with the ability to grow a new brain, we may get to a place where dyslexia can be cured. As of now, no research shows a cure for someone who is struggling with a particular part of the brain is damaged or not normal.

Now, we can look at this brain function as a disadvantage. Or. We can look at this as an advantage.

What are the advantages of the dyslexic brain?

Imagine that we are living in a society that is confusing and pulls us into many different directions all at once.

Not really difficult to imagine.

Now imagine the brain pulling us in many different directions at once.

Imagine one of those directions that just does not pull.

This non-pulling is a huge advantage to the dyslexic brain. How many of us would love it if we could turn off our minds and focus down on a single topic? Or perhaps, one could stop the mind from focusing on a particular intelligence so the other six will grow stronger than normal.

The dyslexic mind, given the freedom to work on other bits of intelligence, does not get distracted by language or reading.

Do we live in a world where we have to know how to read and write? Yes. Is reading and writing the pinnacle of education and intelligence? Currently, yes. Does society look down at those who cannot read and write and calls them names like ignorant or stupid? Unfortunately, yes.

It is up to those who are not linguistically gifted to give themselves a break and not listen to all the above questions.

We also may want to consider that we are a people of diversity. Those who are born with the ability to not be distracted by what others think is important may be the gifted ones. Dyslexia may be a blessing to achieve a higher existence.

And in that, we need to look at what it means to be gifted. Those currently labeled as gifted are the minority. When, in fact, all of us can get to a place where we are superior in any form of intelligence.

And look at that, we are all "gifted."

The mind of a dyslexic is one that can out focus on a mind that is bogged down and working on language and reading. It is only logical to come to the conclusion that those who spread themselves out thinner can be beaten in the specifics of one particular skill. If allowed to see the whole of intelligence, dyslexic mind has an advantage here.

Take reading, for example. Someone who is dyslexic has to concentrate very much on the written word. Those without do not. Eventually, if we are truly looking at the effort of reading, those with dyslexia will outperform those who do not have to utilize effort.

Just like someone who is blind can, more often than not, hear better than those of us who can see.

There are many more advantages to the dyslexic mind than just one concept of intelligence. Perhaps we can leave that up to those who are dyslexic to explain what they are good at. And maybe we can support them in whatever they find to help all of us read better.

In terms of help or healing, we begin to ask the question.

What are some therapeutic pathways we can take?

Therapy is the objective helping of a patient. Since we are working with biological combined with a mental disability, there are multiple pathways to take.

Physically speaking, therapy is to make the body stronger or to heal it. The mind is not an abstract concept. It is right there inside our skulls. It has blood and bone around it. It is made up of materials that make us, us.

To take on dyslexia from a physical position is to take into account activity and nutrition. An inactive body will not produce an active brain. It is shown that some physical activity is needed daily to make the mind improve.

More importantly, there is a position of nutrition. The myths that there are foods that are "brain foods" are common. However, a solid, healthy diet with a combination of energies and flavor is beneficial for the mind to operate at its fullest potential. Solid healthy food leads to a solid healthy mental state.

Never forget the water. Using the mind dehydrates. It is the burning of energy to make the mind work on reading. Yet we ignore that and think that if we are not physically active, we are not burning energy.

Physically speaking around dyslexia, consider the input of sustenance when dealing with the brain. Water and food are directly related to mental issues.

It is the mental side of everything that dyslexia really touch. Let us look at some mental therapy.

Mental therapy is a silver bullet for dyslexia as well as any mental disorder. Yes, science can prescribe mind-altering drugs. Medication may not really be what we need here.

What we need here is to give someone with dyslexia the skills to handle the emotions and logic behind the frustration of not being able to excel at all seven intelligences. These skills stem from mental health therapy.

Mostly when we are talking about mental health, we are working with internal judgment. When we judge ourselves and say we are dyslexic, we are labeling ourselves and making it so that we have judged the situation completely. Mental therapy is about breaking down this judgment into the bones of fact.

Is part of the mind not as developed as others? Yes.

Are we struggling with one of the seven intelligences? Yes.

Do we feel inferior? Yes.

Mental therapy looks at the facts and then determines validity. The mind not being as developed as others begin to take us from fact to social opinion. The struggle is a fact. Feelings are fact and valid, and that covers our feeling of inferiority.

So, really, all we are looking at from a mental health perspective is what skill is needed for the one with dyslexia to understand they are not like everyone else.

These mental health skills can take an entire book to fill. It also takes years to program ourselves to see dyslexia and our relationship to it, as something that needs to be defined by ourselves versus others.

This is the true mental therapy of dyslexia. Do not let anyone use the words, inferior, slow, stupid, or deficit.

For dyslexics are not. Different is not a deficit. Even though those two words look alike. They are not the same. And if you want proof that this rejection of label and name-calling is a mental therapeutic solution to dyslexia, try this.

Take all seven intelligences and write them down.

Find the individual who made the diagnosis of dyslexia. Ask them if they have balance in all seven intelligences.

Most likely, they struggle somewhere.

Then question what is really happening with dyslexia, and why are "learning difficulties" in music, or math, or physical kinesthetic not scientifically explored? If you struggle making music, why is there not a label for that? Or why is everyone making music the social normality?

Why is linguistics the only intelligence that society has attached the word "deficit" to?

Then consider embracing the fact that dyslexics are simply different.

Are you enjoying this book? If so, I'd be really happy if you could leave a short review on amazon, it means a lot to me! Thank you.

CHAPTER 3: THE DYSLEXIA EXPERIENCE

When we are talking about the experience of dyslexia, those with dyslexia say the same thing.

They can read.

It is just that all the letters jump around and goes from recognized word to unrecognized word or possibly another word altogether.

We are talking about a great amount of concentration needed to read here. And that is something that others take for granted. Concentration to do something difficult is something we all understand. Concentration to do something that we all already do is confusing for us.

That confusion is already in the mind of those with dyslexia.

Consider having difficulty with math. You are always without enough money. When you go out to buy something, you lose money because you lose concentration, and it all gets jumbled up.

This inability to concentrate on mathematics when needed can wreck an existence. The inability to concentrate on writing or the sound of language can just as easily wreck a life.

For the individual who has dyslexia, reading is the main issue. Most likely, since reading is so hard to concentrate on, they have developed another form of intelligence that is superior to most as a workaround.

How does someone who struggles with linguistic intelligence get by from day today?

Consider the written word. It is everywhere. Take a drive. Street signs and directions are all in English and are easily navigated. Most read a sign, and it tells them where to go.

Now take a drive in a country that does not speak English.

Road signs are all garbled. Directions are non-existent. Getting lost happens often and is almost expected. Even directions written down by someone who cares is nothing but a garbled mixed-up mess.

This applies to almost anything that someone with dyslexia touches. How much of our intake in everyday life is the written word? Seriously, take a moment and watch some television. Count how many words you see in, say five minutes.

Advertisements, subtitles, closed captions are all filled with the written word. Street signs in an active drive scene. Words on a computer as a person look at information on the show.

What everyone else has set up to be completely entertaining, those with dyslexia, have one of two choices. Struggle to read, or forget about reading altogether.

Either struggling or forgetting about reading during an activity that is supposed to be relaxing is, well, not relaxing.

The struggle does not stop there.

Say the sound of a word comes into the ear of someone with dyslexia and they transpose it with another word, as they do when they see it written.

Now we are talking about the basic ability to communicate with another human being.

How can an artist who thinks blue is red communicate clearly with another artist?

This is something that will get in the way of almost all the other seven intelligences. Imagine having to communicate musically with language. Students and musicians all talk about music all the time. A person with dyslexia will have to concentrate much more than everyone else to have these simple conversations about such a complex topic.

Then there is basic instruction. What if left becomes right? Flipping a switch to the left versus the right may make a series of switches not work. This takes us into the usage of almost all tools, including a computer.

Dyslexics require immense more concentration than those who utilize language more effectively.

Reading and language do not just exist in the classroom. An individual who struggles with linguistics has to find a different pathway to get through the world. Lucky for them and us and everyone around, there are other forms of intelligence, and those tend to find a solution.

The use of getting around the jumbled concentration of reading requires a very creative mind.

The final experience that the dyslexic individual has is that this creative workaround is not always accepted by everyone around them. In other words, conforming to the way everyone else uses language is a one-way street for a person who struggles with linguistics. The person struggling must have patience with those who find language so easy.

One would think that tolerance would be necessary for themselves. This is not the case. Those with dyslexia already have a workaround. Patience for others is a major hurdle. Most likely, those who are linguistically 'deficient,' already have a creative solution for linguistic intelligence and are merely waiting for those who are 'normal' to catch up and try.

Patience is a very useful tool for those who are linguistically challenged. That, combined with the understanding that others are and do not have the same patience, life is more than just communication.

As a Parent

As a parent, a child with dyslexia is going to struggle. Sometimes there is no action to take, and all you can do is feel.

You, as a parent, will experience a different form of anger. However, your anger will be valid and justified only when you discuss it directly with your child. Keeping your anger to yourself will not help your child in any shape, size, or form. You are the communicator that will have the patience to allow the struggling child to get there by showing that you are angry too.

Here is the experience of parents often forgot.

Dyslexia never turns off.

We look to and at our children over and over again, thinking that we are helping them, and then we break. Dyslexia never breaks, and never will. From the perspective of a parent, let us take a look at the difference between understanding a situation and taking action within that situation.

If you are a parent and you are reading this, good on you. Learning is the first step in helping someone who is suffering from linguistics. Here is something that is normally not taught to parents who are dealing with dyslexia.

You are going to feel helpless.

That is because you are. Yes, there are actions to take. The unfortunate bottom line is that language is everywhere; the written word is everywhere; your child is going to struggle for their entire life.

This is a huge feeling of helplessness. No matter how many times you help your child, since dyslexia never turns off, you will never see the completion of help. There will always be a sense of, can you do more.

The best advice is to embrace the creative ways your child gets around this condition. Pride in your child can and will have to be in something other than the traditional sense of what education is. Of what intelligence is. Of what life is.

This means that the way you look at life may have to be re-written for your child. You, as the parent, may have to take on a new creative way of living that is not so focused on the written or spoken word.

The difficulty as a parent will be to take this the other way. To abandon reading is not the answer to dyslexia. Your child can read. It is just difficult for them. They can process information; it just maybe at a slower rate. Do not give up on this form of linguistic intelligence, even if you may feel the need to.

Hopelessness is most likely the biggest hurdle to helping your child. Do not give up. Over-communicate with your child and find out what they need then take action for them.

As a Teacher

As a teacher, the experience you have with dyslexia is one of fact. Understand that one in five students in your classroom has dyslexia. It is just a matter of extremity. Some will be struggling harder than your other students.

So, if you have a class of thirty or more students, no question, one will be dyslexic.

This is alarming because learning is mostly based on language. Yes, students who are dyslexic will excel at different subjects other than those based on reading or writing or speaking. Yet, that is not the real experience of the teacher.

Teachers want to teach everyone.

However, a teacher has to work within the bounds of what is determined by society as education. A very difficult job, indeed, would you not say.

Gaining the attention of thirty minds is difficult. Minds of children are even more difficult. Now consider a child with dyslexia who struggles with language in all forms. How hard is it to get the attention of that child and combine the class?

If the stats are true, and they can be debated, that one child in five has dyslexia, then a teacher is struggling to acquire the attention of seven students in a classroom of thirty-five. And when they consider that dyslexia never stops being dyslexia, there is a difficulty.

The drama of the teacher is not in the inability to reach a child with dyslexia; it is making and teaching the class as a whole. Here is the difficulty of having students with difficulties in linguistic intelligence.

When teaching, in a way that reaches everyone, everyone will have to slow down to the pace of the student who struggles. They say that the weakest link in a chain is the one most stressed. This is true for your students with dyslexia. They will be stressed and want that stress to stop.

Without understanding, other students will start to rebel. Communication with the entire class is an event, whereas patience is required. You the teacher may have all the patience in the world for a student who struggles; however, your students may not. And in that lies the difficulties.

How do you get all the other students to slow down so that the student with dyslexia can keep up? What if it is more than one? What if it truly is more than twenty percent of your class? Do you feel that work handed in with only seventy-eight percentile of completion deserves an A, like only reaching seventy-eight percent of your class? Of course not. You, the teacher, want to teach everyone. To get to one hundred percent of your class is your job and pride.

Deservingly, teachers have the ability to change the world. Frustration in holding back students who are already excelling at reading for a student who struggles with reading is pure drama.

Dyslexia does not go away. And who is to say that the concept of dyslexia can be connected to all the other forms of intelligence. Where one student thrives in language, another may strive in math. What if a student goes to bodily intelligence, and you have no real way of measuring that? Are you going to give a student an A because they are spatially aware? To teach seven different intelligences, to a multitude of individual minds, all mostly with underdeveloped areas is madness.

So, teachers, frustration, yes. Patience required, yes. Understanding, yes.

However, there is a solution. The best classes have a teacher that lets the class teach itself. For example.

As a teacher, most likely, you will have a student (regardless of age) that is more intelligent than you are. Wisdom and education may indeed be on your side; however, there are going to be students who are more intelligent than you are.

When you match a student, who is gifted with linguistics with another student who is struggling with linguistics, watch what happens. It is a job to match difficulty with excellence and vice versa. In essence, you are an adult teaching a child. Getting a child who excels at linguistics to teach a child who struggles will yield greater results than you slowing down the entire class.

This is not to say the solution is to just let all students teach each other. It is a beginning for a student with dyslexia to be matched up with a student who excels at language. It

changes both their lives. And maybe they may whisper se-
crets to each other that they would normally tell an adult. To
read easier and better, maybe in the minds of those trying to
help each other.

Remember, they are under a different pressure than you are
as a teacher. Let them try new concepts.

As an Employer

As an employer, understand this. Those who cannot or struggle with reading are not worthless. In fact, they will excel in
directions your other employees will not. Dyslexic individuals have very much employable skills.

It is your job as an employer to find those skills.

Experiencing dyslexia as an employer may require some patience. This patience is paid upfront. Trust in that those who
suffer dyslexia are already finding a creative way around
their struggle. Eventually, they will find new, better ways to
work.

And here is a point that we may want to stop on. As an employer, you may find that those with dyslexia have found a
better way of doing things. Keeping an open mind may make
the workplace a much better place. Allowing change will
also keep the workplace more productive and more creative.

Employees with dyslexia are going to be gems that sparkle eventually. Consider this by paying a little patience upfront.

Someone who has to struggle their entire life puts in more energy into any subject of skill than someone who does not struggle. Now consider what type of person will be the better employee, those who have overcome the struggle to survive, or those who do not have to.

Let us cut to the chase and let you the employer in on it; those who struggle to overcome will win more often than those who do not. An employee that overcomes dyslexia is prime victory already. It is only up to you as their employer to get over the learning curve to get them into work.

And there is the true experience of dyslexia for an employer. Patience and additional work upfront for someone with dyslexia will excel them past other employees. Yes, those who struggle with linguistics are going to need a little extra to get going.

In addition, they may need a little understanding along the way. They will find their place amongst their peers. And this eventually leads us to the conclusion that people are people regardless of how they are labeled.

The bottom line is that they need to be treated like all other employees. The experience as an employer may have you see the difficulties of intelligence and linguistics with dyslexic employees as something of a setback. Another consideration is that the workplace is just like the classroom. Since dyslexia never goes away, one in five of your workforces has a learning disorder. Pair them up and see what happens.

It is most likely more when we talk about deficits in all six of the other intelligences. We are just talking about linguistic.

Keep that in mind when you are addressing the troops. You, like the teacher, have a job to do that requires some patience and understanding, to get all your troops on the same page.

As a Friend

Friendship is a very unique concept. Most think that friendship has two critical dimensions. Interdependence and voluntary participation are the core of friendship. With dyslexia in mind, we can look at friendship from both sides of the relationship and deal specifically with linguistics.

So, let us break down friendship into its two components and take a look at what dyslexia does to friendship.

Interdependence is for the lack of a better term, dependence on each other. Dependence is the state of relying on each other. In other words, friends rely on each other.

A friend who relies on someone with dyslexia may have to get over some trust issues. When communication breaks down, trust is one of the first things to question. Communication builds trust. With someone who is dyslexic that may prove slow going, or even difficult.

Trust is a concept that those with dyslexia may have to keep in mind when they struggle with their friends. When communication breaks down, a friend may have trouble trusting. This means that those with dyslexia will have to over-communicate with their friends. And those who are friends will have to show some patience when it comes to trust.

The other part of friendship is voluntary participation. When we are talking about voluntary anything, we are talking about free will. We all know what it means to participate in-activity.

At the most basic, we all know to actively participate in the day by getting up. This awakening into reality is participation. We do not have to, yet we willingly do.

It is the free will that makes friendship what it is. Here is the difficulty when we have troubles with dyslexia.

A steady flow of communication will give movement and cause in others to take an active part in anything life has to offer. No one really does anything unless they have made up their minds to do so. In the process of making up their minds, they have listened, learned, and communicated with others. Possibly to the point of writing something down.

Those who are friends with someone who is dyslexic may have to jump out in front from time to time with very little communication involved. What we mean by this is that someone with dyslexia will not be able to communicate need as swiftly as everyone else. Therefore, a friend of someone who struggles with language may have to do some guess-work as to what needs and does not need to be willingly participated in. They may have to forgo the communication process and just willingly participate in the life of those with dyslexia.

The opposite of this is true, as well. It may take painstaking patience to get to what is needed for the friendship from those with dyslexia. This slowing down of communication until everyone is on the same page takes time. So be patient. Those who struggle with the intelligence of linguistics are brilliant and may take time.

Those who struggle with dyslexia and the ability to communicate need only to do this. Focus on your friend more than they focus on you. This may seem an imbalance. It is not. Those who find it hard to communicate will have to be more willing than those who communicate more easily.

This is because when we do not communicate, we do not know what our friends need or want. Sitting quietly with a friend will only go so far. Eventually, their needs are going to have to be looked at and communicated.

For now, at first, those with dyslexia need to work harder on friendship than their friends do.

Considering the difficulties of relationships in this world, the fact that we all speak so many languages and still get along is astounding.

So, there is great hope in friendship and the basic forms required for it to break down our understanding of dyslexia so that it can be built up again. Making and working on friendship may be the silver bullet that heals our intelligent deficits. It is definitely an understanding of each other that occurs when we are trying to be friends. And here is the best part. Everyone gets friendship regardless of language.

Friendship is a world view.

CHAPTER 4: RETRAIN THE BRAIN

Now that we understand, fundamentally, what dyslexia is, how it works, and how it can be experienced by those who have it, we can move forward into applying some effort into helping to compensate and overcome some of the difficulties that dyslexics face.

The Way the Dyslexic Mind Works

One of the most difficult things that those with dyslexia face has come out in the light of new studies. It has been discovered that while it was once thought that dyslexia strictly applied to language, especially where it connects to reading, it has more to do with how the brain does or does not adapt to observations on multiple fronts.

Two separate research studies were conducted by researchers at the Hebrew University of Israel, and one with researchers from MIT that produced very similar results, even though their methods took different approaches.

Earlier in this book we discussed the ability to utilize brain plasticity to help those with dyslexia "rewire" their brains in order to better utilize those areas that could help to create a better comprehension of what they were trying to learn, especially through the way they process things when they read.

This is also known as "neuroplasticity," and it is the brain's ability to adapt and change based on what it experiences, whether that be visual, aural, or oral. For those with dyslexia, this can be a very helpful tool.

Plasticity is not a reference to the brain being like plastic. It was once believed that learning and other external stimuli that created changes or imprints to the brain could only take place from infancy up through childhood. Until more recent studies of the brain through the last several decades, science had determined that that the neural pathways that created the physical "structure" of an individual's brain was pretty much permanent and was finished developing by the time they reached early adulthood.

Plasticity, especially in our discussion of neuroplasticity, actually refers to the brain's ability to be far more malleable than we once thought it was. Our brains continue to create new pathways based on our experiences and can even alter existing pathways to adapt to learning, or re-learn ways to do things, and can even create new memories that aid in our ability to learn.

This newer research that has come to light has brought us even more information as to how the dyslexic mind works by demonstrating that part of the problem that dyslexics face with learning, and comprehension of reading and writing, is because their brains actually have a little less plasticity than found in those who do not have dyslexia.

Both studies performed demonstrated that those who have dyslexia have difficulties in remembering recent events, including images shown to them. Their brains had difficulty adapting to repeated stimuli, which in addition to spoken words, included memory for faces, and even for musical notes.

This type of connection to stimuli is called implicit or incidental memory. It is the premise that recent events or exposure to stimuli are easily forgotten because the brain doesn't make a connection to things that it didn't realize it was supposed to remember when they happen. The imaging done on the brains of those who have dyslexia while the studies took place showed that during these times of implicit memory, the brain does not work as efficiently as do those who do not have dyslexia. The incidental memory fades quickly enough that the brain is not given enough time to adapt, even after the repetition of reading or hearing things. It is part of the reason why reading, spelling, and writing become such hard and slow work for those who are dyslexic. Their brains have to work that much harder to process what it is being exposed to.

In general, the brain is stimulated whenever it is exposed to whatever method of stimuli. It works to understand what it is being exposed to. Once has a brain has been exposed to a particular element, say the sound of a note, it is not as likely to jump into activity the second time that same note is heard because it has already cataloged it in some portion of its memory. It doesn't have to work as hard when it hears the note the second time; it only reacts to capture a little bit more information each time. So, repetition actually helps the brain to relax a little, because it only has to capture any additional information it may have not captured the first time around. Repetition actually helps the brain to become more efficient when it already recognizes something that it has previously been exposed to.

The studies demonstrated that those who have dyslexia have less adaptability, or plasticity with their brains, directly related to shorter, implicit memories. If something was repeated to a person with dyslexia, whether visual or aural, their recall was much better when exposed 3 seconds later, as opposed to 9 seconds later. Such a short time, 6 seconds, and it created difficulty for those with dyslexia to connect to what they were supposed to be focusing on during the study!

The research found that this difficulty in memory was evident whether it was connected to reading, hearing, or other visual stimuli. Further research is in the works to see whether this implicit memory deficit is evident when it comes to other senses experienced by the individual, such as taste or touch. But it has begun to raise a question as to why, if someone with dyslexia has such difficulty with implicit memory, does it manifest itself more readily in reading, writing, and spelling?

Part of that reason, they have conjectured, is that reading, writing, and spelling, this type of communication format that we have developed only in our later years of evolution, primarily utilizes certain portions of the brain. Specifically, for those without dyslexia, the activity is focused more on the rear portions of the brain, while those who have been diagnosed with dyslexia utilize more of the front, left portions of the brain. When it comes to things such as the face or sound recognition, we actually have more neural pathways available for our thoughts to travel and utilize, thus making it far easier for someone with dyslexia to compensate for these types of activities.

What this also tells us is that while there may be less plasticity of the brain for someone who is dyslexic, it is entirely possible for us to help work with someone who has dyslexia, and helps them to rewire the neural pathways in such a way that they can lead successful lives in their future!

There are actually two forms of neuroplasticity. There is structural plasticity, which is described as the brain's ability, or adaptability, to make changes to the physical structure of neural pathways due to the learning processes it is exposed to. This is where most of those who struggle with dyslexia have a difficult time, because of the implicit memory issues that they face.

The second form of neuroplasticity is what they call functional plasticity. This is where the brain has the ability to adapt and move certain functions that a brain would normally perform in one area to another area. This usually happens when a portion of the brain is damaged, and the brain works to move the ability to accomplish things, such as reading or writing from the damaged portion of the brain to an undamaged portion of the brain. In the case of dyslexia, the brain is moving these functions from one area to another, even without the damage being present.

There are a lot of reasons that brain plasticity can be affected. While plasticity can affect the formation and adaptation of neural pathways, it is not actually the neurons that are affected, but rather the brain cells themselves. Thus, plasticity can be affected by age and environmental factors such as genetics, making it a prime target to be affected in those with dyslexia.

So, now we can understand a little better that dyslexia is not just about people reversing letters, numbers, and words, or seeing them backward or jumbled. Reversing letters is actually normal in the developmental process, and happens to most children up through the first or second grade.

One of the biggest problems that dyslexics face is that they struggle with connecting the symbols of letters and/or words to the basic understanding of the sound they are supposed to produce. This process involves the building blocks of words themselves, the sounding out of the letters to combine and form a word, and is known as phonemes (FO-neems). Just connecting the individual sounds that each letter makes becomes difficult, let alone combing these sounds together into a word.

Because it takes time for someone with dyslexia to connect these symbols to sounds and pronounce them together as a whole word, their short-term memory affected by the implicit memory, causes them to struggle time and time again, often leading them back to the beginning to start from scratch. The time it takes for the struggling connection that they have, and need to make for reading comprehension, causes them to "lose" the word they were struggling with, and they have to start over again from the beginning. How frustrating!

But with proper help, and the right way found for their brain to connect with the words, letters, and symbols, we now know that it is possible to find ways to help them through their struggles.

Understanding How to Work with the Dyslexic Brain

Most of us begin to learn how to read in the same way. We learn our ABCs. We then learn how each of those letters (and combinations of letters) has a sound that is attached to them. This is called phonemic awareness. Once we get the hang of this, we move on to phonics (part of what we already described as phonemic awareness), and we learn how to take these separate sounds and blend them together to make full words. Eventually, this enables us to sound out words we may not have seen before but sometimes find that we have already heard.

Reading can be difficult even for those who are beginning without the struggle of dyslexia. It takes time. It takes practice. It takes repetition. With these three things, we gradually develop the ability to read the words we are learning automatically. This step allows us to then move on to actually comprehending what it is we are reading because now our mental energy resources have been freed up from the initial steps.

What happens for those with dyslexia, however, is that because they struggle with phonemic awareness and the concept of phonics, that step of automatically reading a word and having the brain energy available for comprehension doesn't happen. Instead, their brain energy is continually focused on their struggle with the beginning steps of trying to recognize letters and then attached sounds to them and then sound the word out. For someone who has more trouble than the rest with implicit, short-term memory, if not given proper ways to work with their understanding process, they will continue to struggle for the rest of their life.

In addition, there are sometimes the mix up of letters and backward words that, while others grow out of, those with dyslexia often do not. Sometimes they lose the spaces between words, so their brain may interpret two words as being one long word, adding to the difficulty. So, their reading comprehension is punctuated even further by beginning level struggles that the rest of those their age may have already surpassed.

If you are already struggling with the drawn-out chore of sounding letters and words out, it doesn't help with the ability to retain and comprehend what was just read, either. Life becomes a long struggle of frustration.

Those who struggle with dyslexia start to feel that they are not smart, or at the very least, not as smart as those with whom they are learning alongside. Since reading and reading comprehension plays such a large part in the learning process, their struggles and frustrations can grow through the years of school.

Often, when you are not good at something, you avoid doing it. Especially if it appears that you will never get any better at it. For those with dyslexia, they stop or avoid reading because it is hard from them, and creates a great deal of stress for them. This causes them to miss out on the opportunity to practice their reading skills toward improvement, and they can fall even further behind.

Reading is a workout that exercises your brain on multiple levels. When we read, we are actually completing a complex series of steps, and it all happens at once. For those who don't have dyslexia, the completing of all of these steps becomes second nature, a simple task that we rarely have to focus on anymore. For those who struggle with dyslexia, it is a complex nightmare of frustration that stops them from being able to move to the next level of reading comprehension.

When we read, this is what our brains are doing, all at the same time:

1. We are processing the knowledge that words are comprised of a series of sounds.
2. We look at the printed letters or numbers on a page and focus on each one.
3. We start to recognize and connect sounds to each letter.
4. We blend the sound of each letter into a combination of sound that creates a word.
5. We move our eyes in a controlled manner across the page.
6. The comprehension of each word, and then the words combined together into a thought, starts to build ideas and/or images in our mind.
7. Our brains take new information and store it, or takes information and compares it to what is already stored and keeps those parts that it had not stored before.

When you struggle with those beginning stages, such as those who have dyslexia do, the rest of the steps are even harder to achieve, if even possible. It is enough to make anyone's brain quickly reach a point of being tired, let alone someone who has to struggle every step of the way.

Because of this on-going struggle, in addition to having trouble with the actual learning process, those with dyslexia can become frustrated. They can have difficulties being expressive because they lack the language connection. This can develop into low self-esteem. Depression and stress make their struggles even more difficult, seemingly insurmountable.

One of the first things you can do when working with someone who struggles with dyslexia is to help them understand that there is nothing wrong with them and help them to believe in themselves again. In and of itself, support for someone who is struggling can make all the difference in the world in their willingness to pick themselves back up, shake, and brush the dust off and start again.

Changing Perceptions and the Way You (and They) Think

The first thing we need to remember is that dyslexia is not just about the way the brain processes language. It does have that as a part of a whole, to be sure. But the truth is that the brain of someone with dyslexia just works differently than that of the norm, and that is not necessarily a bad thing!

As was previously noted, linguistics/language is not the only part of our brains that has earned the term "intelligence." We have multiple ways that our brains process things and many ways in which intelligence can be measured, not just through the written word. It is far better to look upon dyslexia as a difference, rather than a deficit or a disability.

Just because an individual doesn't excel in the classroom, with high marks in reading, writing, and spelling, there are many other ways to encourage the learning process and help to rewire the brain for success. Someone with a lack of high scores in the areas of linguistics may be shown to have extremely high marks in the areas of visual/spatial intelligence. Many of those with dyslexia have scored high in these areas that mark creativity and "outside the box" ways of thinking. These are trademarks of artists such as Andy Warhol, Leonardo DaVinci, and Jackson Pollack.

Because of the restricting "pigeon-holing" of educators for those who struggle with dyslexia, many leave the world of academia behind and push out on their own, utilizing their other strengths to the best of their abilities. Three very successful dyslexics who pursued businesses that allowed them to show their creative talents, alongside their abilities of problem-solving and sheer determination, are (were) Alan Sugar (the British business magnate of the Amstrad empire), Richard Branson, and Steve Jobs.

There are even highly successful dyslexic authors who worked hard to overcome their difficulties with the hardest of tasks for someone with dyslexia… linguistic comprehension. But their struggle to write is far overshadowed by the uniqueness of their groundbreaking stories put to paper. These authors, such as George Bernard Shaw, Agatha Christie, WB Yeats, F. Scott Fitzgerald, John Irving, Jules Verne, Roald Dahl, and so many others were successful because their dyslexic brains looked at things just differently enough to create amazing, spell-binding tales.

It is these differences that we must celebrate and help those who struggle with dyslexia to understand as a positive rather than a negative. If we are going to continue to judge the intelligence of those around us by the simplistic, standardized testing performed in schools to gauge skills at mathematics and linguistics, then we set a low standard for ourselves as a race moving forward.

It is possible for many dyslexics to overcome the challenges in reading and writing in an academic setting. But we need to stop thinking of dyslexia as being a limitation. And we need to help those who struggle with dyslexia to understand that they are not limited to a life of struggle that they can overcome or move past the struggle and onto something that they will excel at.

The idea here is not only to help those who struggle with dyslexia to find ways to cope or compensate for the way that their brains work in order to progress academically. We must also learn how to give them messages of encouragement for the unique ways that they think, and that they should actively seek to embrace their creativity instead of quelling it. By turning the dialog into something positive, instead of refer-ring to it as a disability or deficit, we take the first step to-ward encouragement and raising levels of self-esteem. With encouragement, we start those who struggle with dyslexia on a different path... one of exploration for the amazing things that they can accomplish in life.

It can be true that those with dyslexia often struggle with the difficulties with which they are faced. Through support and encouragement, they can continue to conquer these difficul-ties, and learn that with persistence, any setback can be over-come. When faced with something they may feel as an inad-equacy when compared to others, we can teach them how to look at their problems from a variety of angles to come up with innovative solutions. This leads them to become natural problem solvers as they grow and develop.

Sometimes the need to step back and read and re-read things also gives a different perspective than others may see. It is the creation and expansion of something that an individual going through something once may never reach because they are already on to the next best thing. Being dyslexic may be a struggle, but just because something is hard, or we have a hard time grasping it at first, that is far from being a failure. It means that your successes are worth that much more because of what you had to endure to get there. This is the message that we need to be retraining ourselves to think, and how we must approach those dyslexics in our lives.

So yes, it is important, especially because of the way schools are academically set up, to help the dyslexic individual in your life to overcome some of the struggles they face with reading, writing, and spelling. This is a necessary and helpful tool for them to have in their toolbelt regardless of the rest of the future they will be facing, no matter the path they eventually choose to follow. We will be going over some ways that you can help the dyslexic individual in your life to succeed on multiple levels, starting in the next chapter.

But to help build confidence and self-esteem to make their enthusiasm for learning a little higher, it may help to start working with them to find out what other areas they may excel in, and help them to find their successes in those areas that will carry their self-confidence back into the academic areas where they also need to work.

With the multitude of problems that the world faces today, we have a great need for minds that can think outside the box. The standard ways of thinking, conforming to a set of rules to make everyone think in the same way is not going to be what gets us through the future. The dyslexics in our lives may just be the ones to get us there, to having the promise of a future at all.

Instead of focusing on the "deficit" of being dyslexic, we need to be focusing on how we can help those with dyslexia realize their true potential, and use their creative energy, imagination, and problem-solving skills to move into whatever dream they want to chase.

Remember… there is more than just linguistic/language intelligence. There are those intelligences within us that govern art and creativity, communication, numbers and reasoning, musicality, personal awareness, body awareness, and fine and gross motor skills. Where does it say that someone can only succeed if they can read at a standardized level? It will definitely aid them in moving forward, but it does not have to stop them from pursuing any dream they choose to dream.

As mentioned above, there have been authors, artists, and business individuals who have succeeded in their chosen career paths, despite, or some say even because of their dyslexia. There also athletes, such as football players Alex Green, Mark Schlereth, and Frank Gore… baseball player Jeremy Bonderman… basketball players Jewell Lloyd and Magic Johnson… boxer great Muhammad Ali… Meryl Davis, a two-time Olympic ice skater… And even New York Jets coach Rex Ryan… These are all famous athletes who struggled with dyslexia and went on to become incredible players in our history of sports.

Some of the science greats were dyslexic as well, including Alexander Graham Bell, Galileo Galilei, Michael Faraday, Pierre Curie, Jacques Dubochet, Carol W. Greider, and Thomas Alva Edison, just to name a few of the more well-known ones. There have even been actors and actresses who have stepped up to let the world know that they are dyslexic, ad yet have gone on to have some prominent careers... James Oliver, Jennifer Anniston, Keira Knightly, and Orlando Bloom are among them. But in addition to the famous, there are many people who have struggled with dyslexia and have gone on to become successful lawyers, doctors, and statesmen of our time.

Dyslexia is considered a learning disability, but it does not have to be a lifelong sentence of holding back. With dedication and hard work, it can become a tool rather than prevention to use with the strength of other abilities, including perseverance.

CHAPTER 5: HOW YOU CAN HELP

As was started to be examined in the previous chapter, one of the first things we can do to help someone in our lives who struggles with dyslexia is to boost their self-esteem, and help them to understand that dyslexia does not have to be seen as a deficit, but it can be an advantage when they play to their strengths.

Each of us likely has someone who struggles with dyslexia in our lives, even though we may not even know it. Dyslexia is not something that someone you meet comes up and introduces themselves, "Hi, I'm John, and I have dyslexia." More likely, because of the troubles they have faced in their lives, or are facing now, they try to hide their dyslexia from those they encounter, and as adults, many have become very adept at doing just that.

Even so, if we pay attention to some of the signs and symptoms of dyslexia, we can help in ways they may not have even realized were available options. So, we're not going to just cover how to help the dyslexic child in your life from the perspective of being a parent or teacher, but we will also touch upon being able to help someone with dyslexia even as a friend or co-worker/employer.

One newer to the scene charitable organization, "Made by Dyslexia," has been formed for the sole purpose of bringing the understanding of dyslexia and how it works to the world, with one target being our schools. Their goal is to make it possible for children to be identified at an early age for dyslexia and being able to get them the proper coping skills and understanding that they need to succeed and thrive in the world today.

There are definitely many more advantages available today for those who struggle with dyslexia than there were even a few decades ago. The technological advances made over the last few decades and have exponentially increased in use even over the past decade can offer many great advantages to those who struggle with dyslexia.

The focus on handwriting, for instance, has shifted, not only in the workplace, but among friends, family, and even in schools. Computers have become the "go-to" for many, which includes word processing, e-mails, and even text messaging. All of these have spell check and even grammar options. This allows for someone with dyslexia to enter the world of the written word far more easily and with less scrutiny or condemnation than they have been exposed to in the past.

With computer use comes keyboard skills, which now, instead of having to recall how each word is formed coming onto the screen, a certain element of touch or muscle memory comes into play, utilizing different portions of the brain than the usual reading and writing portions. Many of our devices now have the text-to-speech options that allow for dyslexics to speak what they want to write, instead of struggling through the writing process as a whole. In addition, reading has been made much easier, with audiobooks for pleasure, and podcasts and computer programs that read the written word out loud from the screen. All of these pieces of technology have helped the world become a far more dyslexia-friendly place to exist.

Still, there are many other ways in which dyslexics can be helped to enhance their performance, develop coping skills, and succeed in various aspects of life. Below are ways that can help, taken from different aspects of life exposure.

As a Parent

As a parent, when you first find out that your child has dyslexia, it can be troubling, and you will naturally want to do everything in your power to help your child. Reading this book is a great first step toward that. One of the best things that you can do is to find out everything that you can about what dyslexia is, how it works, and how it affects the way your child thinks, processes things, and ultimately struggles.

Once you discover what dyslexia is all about, and all of the options available for you to be able to help, it can help relieve some of your fears, which ultimately gets you into the proper place to be able to help your child succeed. It also allows you to make informed choices on which directions you want to take while helping your child, which is an extremely important consideration!

After learning more about dyslexia, your next important step is to work with your child's school as closely as possible, to ensure that the proper resources and services are in place for your child's academic success. Since dyslexia has been discovered to be much more common than once thought, there has been a push for resource availability in schools to help those who struggle with dyslexia.

One of these available options that should be strongly looked into and encouraged is the development of an Individualized Education Plan (IEP), which usually involves a support team consisting of the parent(s), teachers, and counselors who work to guide the educational needs and resources available for your child. This allows for additional considerations to be made for your child concerning classroom accommodations and any other necessary support needed to facilitate a better learning environment for success.

If you feel that your child's needs are not being appropriately met, you may consider asking about what the qualifications of the teachers are at the school that will offer the proper support for your child's learning. If necessary, you may want to look into schools that do have the proper programs designed for the education of dyslexic children. There may also be weekend or summer education reading programs available as an option.

Whatever path you choose to pursue, the earlier you begin, the better it will be for your child's success. Always remember that it is not easy for your child and that they are not only struggling with the academic issues of reading and writing as a dyslexic but also with their self-esteem and confidence levels. Working with them to achieve academic success should not be your only goal. Yes, it is important to focus on routine and schoolwork; but just as important is the need for your child to be shown love, encouragement, support, and above all… patience.

Keep an eye out for signs that your child is frustrated, angry, becoming withdrawn, or feeling periods of low-self-esteem. Any attempts to improve their learning abilities in reading or writing are going to be more difficult if they are in a vulnerable emotional place where they feel they won't be able to succeed.

Avoid making any comparisons with other children or siblings. Those who struggle with dyslexia already feel bad about themselves because they don't feel that they measure up. It is not a contest. Let them know that you aren't expecting them to compete, but rather to succeed on their own terms.

Reading. Just as every person who struggles with dyslexia does so at varying levels of severity, so also, is each child or individual differs in the way that they learn and process things. Each of our strengths is different, and you need to use what you do know about your child's strengths to give them the best chance to succeed, moving forward. There is no "one size fits all" approach, but almost all of the best chances of success involve developing a routine, a lot of practice, support, and love. If you have a hard time figuring out ways to tackle all of this on your own, perhaps speaking with your child's school counselor or even a psychologist may help you to formulate the best plan that you can help apply to your child and reinforce in their routine.

When it comes to reading, one thing that helps stands out above the rest... Read. Read. Read. Read Again. Read a lot. Of course, there are multiple ways that you can approach reading with your child.

Audiobooks are a great option to get your child reading. Use the audiobook alongside the print book. While the audiobook is running, have your child read alongside it, so they learn to more easily recognize words as they are being sounded out by someone else, instead of simply struggling to sound out each word themselves.

Encourage your child to spend time reading on their own, practicing both quiet reading, as well as readings out loud.

Go back and re-read the child's favorite books. While it may get boring for you, this helps them to better focus on the reading, since the comprehension of the story being told is already there.

Take turns with your child, reading books out loud together. Again, this helps them to better focus on the reading and recognition of the words because they have already achieved a level of comprehension from hearing you read.

Engage your child's comprehension of what is being read by discussing what you are reading. Ask them questions along the lines of, "That was exciting... what do you think is going to happen next?"

When you have read something with your child, try sketching a little image next to the point or paragraph that helps show what the reading was about. This helps when they are reviewing or re-reading information to bring better recall and comprehension.

Sometimes those who have dyslexia have difficulty with the white glaring background that most written words are printed on. Try printing out reading material on colored paper. If in a book, or a worksheet or other printed pages that come from a different source like school, then try getting some colored acetate sheets (see-through plastic) to put over the page and see whether that helps improve their ability to read.

Don't just focus on school books. Yes, reading school books with your child are necessary for their academic work, but you want to engage them in reading. Sometimes comic books or graphic novels can be a great way to encourage your child's reading because the images help to convey comprehension and can make reading more fun.

When your child is reading, try having them use their finger or a card or piece of paper to cover up the word and only reveal it in small pieces, helping them to separate the whole word out instead of it being one big, overwhelming chunk.

Show your child by example that reading is something you do too. While your child spends time reading, set aside time for yourself to read as well.

Also, try reading in short bursts, and then take a break. Those who are dyslexic use a lot of extra brain energy than others because of their struggle to read and comprehend. Don't try to force long sessions; it will only make your child tired and frustrated. Take breaks and do other activities before coming back to it again. This can also be done by letting your child read in short bursts and then have you take over for a while, discussing what was read in-between. But it really will help to take short breaks away from it all throughout the learning and reading process.

Spelling. Spelling can be very difficult for those with dyslexia, and the traditional methods of teaching spelling still used in schools do not help with the way the dyslexic brain processes things. So, you may have to try a few different methods to help your child gear up for success in spelling.

When working through even simple words, such as "tent," try to work through the separation of the word as a whole to get to the actual pronunciation. For example, pronounce "tent" as "t...ent." This helps to separate what would normally be a single syllable into separate syllables that help to break the word down for better understanding. This can be especially helpful for those words with silent letters, or for longer words that break down oddly, like "W-ed-nes-day".

Like with the reading suggestion, try connecting a picture to what you are trying to help your child spell, especially if it is something they commonly misspell. For example, the word "of," which is often misspelled, "uv". UV is a common connection to the rays of the sun, so maybe drawing a pair of sunglasses on the word "of." Or perhaps the word "first," which is often changed to "ferst." In this case, you may wish to draw a picture of the letter "I" winning a race, which helps your child to recall that "I comes First."

Mnemonics can be a useful tool as well, especially when it comes to spelling. Create a phrase that uses the first letters to create the word you are trying to help your child remember how to spell. For example, to help your child remember how to spell "who," use a phrase such as "Wendy Hates Onions." It can further help if you attach an image to it of a little girl (Wendy) holding an onion and making a face. Another method uses the first word of the phrase as the word you are trying to help your child remember how to spell... "Does" can become, "Does Ollie Eat Strawberries?" Again, an imaged attached of a little boy (Ollie) eating a strawberry, can help to bring further connection and recall.

Writing. Before actually spending time writing out words, it can help your child to get a grasp on forming their thoughts before outing them to paper. Try reading a short passage or thought, and then ask your child to explain what you just read to them in just a few words. This not only helps them with comprehension of spoken words but also helps them to identify and explain what they just heard, formulating it into a thought.

Try helping your child to formulate what they are going to write through the use of keywords. Discuss a concept, and work with them to identify what the keywords of the concept are, and write them down. Now have them write a sentence using those keywords to explain the concept. Cross off each keyword as it is used.

As mentioned at the beginning of this chapter, technology has made great strides in assisting those with dyslexia. Try having a discussion with your child's teacher(s) about allowing your child to turn in their homework, especially written assignments, from a word processing program. This will help them to learn their spelling by the corrections noted by the program, and help with more legible writing assignments.

Memory. It has been shown that dyslexics respond with better recall when presented with pictures or images. When you have words or concepts that you want to get across and have remembered, try using images to help with your child's recall.

Those with dyslexia also struggle with multiple steps. Any time you want to give them a series of tasks to do, try breaking it down into two steps at a time. Wash your hands and brush your teeth. Put your books away and wash your hands. You can help increase the recall by either having your child repeat the steps back to you in order, or helping them to visualize the steps you want them to perform.

Organize. It can help if you work with your child to organize their learning process. Routine can be very important because it helps to set the mood for the brain to go into learning mode. Try creating a routine for your child's learning that you can follow through on through the day or week.

Work with your child and their teacher to create checklists of things that need to be done. This can go hand in hand with creating routines, especially if there are specific assignments that teachers like to see handed in at the same time every week, such as vocabulary lists.

Check with your child's teacher to set up an audio device so that your child can record what is being taught by the teacher so that they can have access to repetitive listening until they can reach comprehension of what is being said. This can also help you to identify what is being taught and where your child is struggling. It allows you to open up a dialog with your child about what they are hearing as opposed to what is being said so that they can gain a better understanding. This will also help your child when it comes to studying for tests, having the verbal information available to them instead of only struggling to go through written information as to their only resource for study.

Try color-coding your child's tasks and assigning times to colors, so that even if the actual assignments change, the same type of assignment is focused on for a certain amount of time every day, and they can see it at a glance and identify it by color.

Set up a place where tools, books, etc. get put away after their study or learning time is done so that it is easily located the next day or the next time that they go to use it. This helps decrease frustration and stress of trying to find what they need when it is time for them to turn their attention toward learning and studying. It can also help to make sure that space, where they study, is free from distractions, as those with dyslexia are often more sound and movement sensitive than others.

Help Make Learning Fun. Anytime you can create a situation of less stress or pressure, it can help your child relax into the learning process. If your child is struggling to remember or comprehend what they are trying to learn, trying utilizing some other options that engage other strong suits that may help them.

Try making up songs to help remember things. You could also try making up poems or even dances that help either to remember or comprehend certain concepts.

Try playing word games. Say a word and then spell it. Ask the child to say a rhyming word and then spell it, for example. The more fun and sillier, the better it will help them to remember. Laughter has been shown to increase out memory retention.

Find some things that your child enjoys and is good at... crafts, cooking, music, art, sports... Allow your child to spend time in these pursuits at least every week. This helps to contribute to their self-esteem and confidence. When possible, include some of the learning in that activity. If your child likes to cook, take the time to find recipes with them, and go over reading them before starting into actually making the recipe. If your child loves art, work with them to create the little images that may help them to identify words and concepts that they struggle with. If your child is into watching a particular sport, go to the website of their favorite team and use reading about the players and stats as part of their learning process.

There is also the option of working with your child through specialized reading and development programs that specifically target assistance with those who have reading or learning disorders, including dyslexia. Some of these include she Orton-Gillingham Approach, The Lindamood-Bell Program, The Wilson Method, RAVE-O, and Preventing Academic Failure (PAF). All of these have proven methods for working toward academic success when faced with learning disabilities. If you decide this may be helpful, then research them and decide which one might best suit the way that your child learns.

As a Teacher

As a teacher, it can be difficult to assess and help each individual student, especially when class sizes have become so large. The option of one-on-one teaching becomes difficult at best. It can also be difficult for a teacher to understand that the student they may consider not putting for an effort, or is careless with their work may actually be dyslexic. And it's not up for teachers to make a diagnosis on any child's potential learning disability. However, teachers are becoming more informed as to what they can watch for as signs that may point to a learning disability and can open a dialog with parents about it with a parent-teacher meeting or conference.

A big part of a teacher's job is to ensure that the classroom is a conducive learning environment for every child assigned to them. This means that every child should be made to feel comfortable in learning and that they develop confidence and self-esteem, rather than feeling singled out or picked on. Every classroom should be a positive learning environment.

It does help when teachers are aware of what they are facing when they have a dyslexic child in the classroom. Now that it has played that one in five children struggle with some varying level of dyslexia, it shows that it is more likely that teachers will encounter at least one child in their teaching career that will have dyslexia. Educators are learning more about what they can do when faced with this struggle by a child under their educational care. It will help them further if they work to increase their knowledge and understanding of what dyslexia is and how it can affect the learning process.

Teachers often teach by speaking to their class. It is only becoming more recently understood that those who have dyslexia struggle with short term memory issues, especially when expressed to them via auditory delivery. This creates troubles not only with sounding out words and sentences but also with comprehension of what is being heard, as well as poor recall when trying to attempt even shortlists of directions.

In the Classroom. It is helpful for all children, but especially those who struggle with dyslexia, to increase repetition in classroom teaching and discussions. It can go a long way to give an outline of what is going to be taught, engage in teaching the subject, and then give a recap of what was taught at the end. This can help increase memory retention of the subject matter.

If you have a child diagnosed with dyslexia or one who consistently has trouble with homework, one thing that can help is to make sure that assignments are written down correctly and that the child has the appropriate books and worksheets or other assignments with them when they go home.

Have the child write down the number of a couple of friends in the front of their notebook or workbook so that if they struggle with remembering what assignments were given, they can contact their friends to remove guessing from the equation.

Make sure that class schedules and messages are not only delivered orally but are written down.

Encourage daily routines to enable self-confidence and repetition learning. Help the child by working to create a daily checklist for work and subject matter that they can use at home that evening.

Work with the child to organize their classwork into separate folders, maybe even color-coding them by class to encourage more responsibility and self-reliance.

Break larger learning tasks down into smaller ones that can be tackled one at a time, and are written down so that none of the steps will be missed.

If the child struggles with poor visual memory, then notetaking and copying things from the blackboard may not be as useful as having handouts or notes available.

Try to have the child sit closer to the teacher or a helpful classmate so that if they are struggling, it will be far easier to help.

Blackboard or Whiteboard Information. Make sure, when writing things for children to copy or learn from the black (or white) board, that the words you write are well spaced so that they are easily distinguished from each other.

Use different color chalk or marker for each line of text that you write, to help distinguish them from each other. Another thought is to use different color chalk or marker to create an underlined space after every second line of text.

Make sure, especially if the information is supposed to be copied down by the child, that it is left on the blackboard for long enough that they have time to copy it down, even when struggling. Another thought is to have the information available via notes that the child can be handled so that they do not have to struggle so hard with copying the information down.

Reading. Having routine and structure to the child's reading environment is important. Take the time to introduce new words slowly and allow them to develop a comfortable level of confidence with them before moving to the next.

If a child has to work and struggle to read, their comprehension of what is being read will be lost in the struggle. This creates a situation where they will not feel the motivation to move forward and progress with their reading. Try to not have the child read anything beyond their reading level.

For a dyslexic child, trying to read something out loud can be very demoralizing. Try to avoid having dyslexic children in your class; read out loud in front of their peers. If necessary, you can have them read out loud to you during some one-on-one time, or perhaps try giving the child the passage to read a day in advance so they can practice reading it out loud at home before they have to read it in front of the rest of the class.

Spelling. It helps those with dyslexia if their lists of spelling words center around a topic, but it helps even more so when these words are grouped in a structure-based format. A few random words can be thrown in to help with free-writing skills.

Teach spelling rules that can help dyslexic children to understand structure when it comes to learning how to spell new words.

Proofreading is a helpful skill for all children. For the dyslexic child, they struggle with the ability to correct themselves while they are writing. As they develop, and they have common mistakes that they continually make, it can help to show them how to proofread for these mistakes specifically.

Mathematics. Mathematics is a language all of its own, which can create its own special problems for a child who has dyslexia. Although there are some dyslexic children who excel at math, studies have shown that almost 90% of dyslexic children struggle in some areas of mathematics. Once they can grasp the basic concepts of what is supposed to be done, i.e., add, subtract, etc. They can have a better grasp of math equations. But many still tend to struggle when doing equations that take longer, multiple steps, such as long divisions, or algebra.

Using estimation skills can be helpful when teaching dyslexic child math. They should always be encouraged to check their answers against an estimate of what the answer should be. This can help them rule out answers that went totally sideways in their processing of the equation.

When teaching children to do math in their heads (mental mathematics), allow a child with dyslexia to write down the key numbers and the mathematical sign appropriate to the equation.

Try encouraging the student to walk through the steps of the problem they are working on out loud. This can help them to formulate the thought behind the process they are trying to perform.

Teach a dyslexic child how to use a multiplications table, and help him to work through the table out loud while using it.

Encourage the use of a calculator with a child who struggles with dyslexia. Make sure to teach them how to work through the estimation process in checking their work.

If the child struggles with the decimal point, try using red ink for the decimal point alone to allow for a better visual connection.

Handwriting. Work with a dyslexic child on their handwriting, helping them to make their own decision as to be critical of their handwriting. Sometimes a more cursive, connected style of handwriting works better for those who are dyslexic.

Work with the child to demonstrate common mistakes when writing words. Write these on the board, or make a note sheet in the front of their workbook. Let them use that sheet to make corrections to mistakes themselves before turning work in.

Make sure that a dyslexic child has a reference sheet to look at for writing both upper case and lower-case letters, especially when working with cursive.

When practicing handwriting, try to use words that the child doesn't already struggle within spelling or reading.

Marking Papers. Marking papers is usually done based on achievement. For the dyslexic child, it is also helpful to mark for effort as well, to help boost their self-confidence. When marking creative writing papers, a lot of consideration should be given to content, not just accuracy in writing.

When marking for spelling, those errors pointed out should be those that match the child's spelling level. Giving positive comments or encouragement can be helpful, as well.

For a dyslexic child, the red ink stands out as a failure, even more so than others, especially when they have to work that much harder to achieve decent grades. Try marking their papers in pencil as opposed to red ink.

Try to avoid having a dyslexic child rewrite any piece of work. They have already put a great deal of effort into its creation, and having to rewrite everything on which they worked so hard can be extremely demoralizing. Only have them rewrite work that may be displayed to others.

Homework. For a dyslexic child, try to only give homework assignments that will really benefit them. They are usually far more tired at the end of the day than their peers because their brains struggle extra hard with processing everything they need to in order to keep up in the classroom.

With that being said, if you are lessening the homework load of a dyslexic child, or giving them something a little different to work on than you do to their peers, try to be circumspect about it. The last thing a dyslexic child needs is the hit to their self-esteem that they are being treated differently than the others in their class. Remember… it is already going to be more difficult for them to complete any homework assignment because they have to work harder at it than the others around them.

Try to keep in mind that it is going to take far longer for dyslexic children to complete the same homework someone else in the classroom may easily finish.

Integrating the Needs of the Dyslexic Child. As just noted, one of the biggest things a teacher is going to need to look at with having a dyslexic child in the classroom is that extra time may need to be allocated for the child to complete the same work as others in their class. They spend additional time struggling with reading, and then planning what they need to do, writing, proofreading, and rewriting, where to some children they can perform this series naturally, without a second thought to the entire process.

You may wish to investigate some of the special methods used by professionals for the teaching of dyslexic children and integrate them wholly into classroom teaching. You never know when some of your other students may benefit from having teaching approached in a different way.

Flexibility in your teaching methods is necessary when dealing with having a child with dyslexia in your class. Maybe instead of having your dyslexic students write a paper, they can give you their assignment orally, so you can be assured that they have a full grasp of the concepts they are being taught. This can also include the ability for the child to turn in papers done on a word processor instead of being hand-written, or taping class sessions so that audio records are available for the child to study.

Regardless of who is in your classroom, the creation of an environment that serves the educational needs of every child in your care is essential to their later successes in life.

As an Employer

As an employer, you are not likely going to immediately know that one of your employees is or may be dyslexic. In today's modern age, there are still adults who have not been actually diagnosed with dyslexia, and with so much information only now coming to light through research and studies are done, they may consider themselves slow, or unintelligent, when nothing may be farther from the truth.

Having an individual with dyslexia working for you may actually be a great advantage rather than a disadvantage. Dyslexic thinkers have proven themselves in business time and again to be creative, outside the box thinkers with incredible problem-solving skills. What they do need from you is the support that can help them effectively do their job.

It first helps to understand how dyslexia might present itself in your employees. There are no visible signs in the way of physical telltales, so it becomes harder to tell whether you might have someone with dyslexia working for you. Some of the problem areas you might notice, such as inconsistent or poor spelling issues, difficulties with following written instructions or directions, having a hard time following step-by-step processes or directions, a disorganized work area or desk, poor time management or timekeeping skills, or difficulty with taking notes for meetings or phone calls. Other indicators can be individuals who call in sick to work regularly, which can often happen with an open office plan that allows for noise and movement distractions or turning down opportunities to be promoted because of the increase of paperwork that may come with the promotion.

It can mean some challenges, such as a slower ability to grasp new changes, which can equate to additional training required when learning new tasks. One of the first things you can work with is to learn how your employee best communicates, and then work to adapt your communication style so that they can better understand what is expected of them.

Each person with dyslexia processes things differently. Some have strong suits in some areas and less so in others. Some individuals may need a demonstration to fully understand what you are trying to get across. Some dyslexics do process verbal directions well, while others do not. Visual, written directions might be a preferred method of communication, so they have something to refer back to. If someone is a visual learner, you may take the time to go over written directions and highlight key points that they need to pay attention to. Flow charts, checklists, or mind maps can be valuable to a visual learner as well.

If they do respond well to verbal instruction, perhaps leaving a detailed voicemail could be an option. That way, again, there is something for them to refer back to again and again, without feeling that they are outing you out by asking you to repeat directions or instructions.

Since reading is often a struggle for those with dyslexia, especially because letters and numbers tend to "move" on the page, you may work with them to find out whether a colored paper may help to bring the letters and numbers into better focus with less difficulty. If they do not already have a preference for color, you can work with them to find a color that suitably benefits their ability to read.

This can also apply to make adjustments on their computer, so things like their word processing backgrounds have a color other than white that allows them to better process the written word. Another consideration is to change the font face they use. Certain font faces seem to work better for those with dyslexia. To really go the extra mile, there are fonts designed specifically to be dyslexic friendly, such as Open-Dyslexic or Dyslexie.

It helps to keep any directions or instructions simple and precise. Deliver them in a quieter area, free from sound distraction, if possible. Again, follow-up with written instructions, so they have something to refer back to.

Allow your employees to record meetings or instructions, so they have a verbal record to refer back to. This can be especially helpful for those who have difficulty keeping track of the written word. In addition, providing a copy of the meeting notes to them in advance will allow them to process better what is being said while actually sitting in on the meeting.

Word processors are often already in use in the workplace, which can be of benefit to a dyslexic employee who needs to write, but also consider speech recognition software as an option, or text readers with headphones, so that employees who do better through auditory instruction or learning have the opportunity to use these. If there are certain words that are consistently misspelled, add the top 50 or so of those to the autocorrect function of the word processor, to help more speedily get through writing.

When providing instructions, notes, or other forms of writing to your employee, avoid using all CAPS, underling, or even italics for emphasis. These cause the shape of the words to change and can make it more difficult for your employees to read. Instead, try using bold letters when you feel the need to provide emphasis.

If handwriting is necessary for your business process, try offering your employee gel pens as opposed to fine line or ballpoint. Gel pens tend to create thicker text, which allows for more control when writing things out by longhand.

Dyslexia is a learning disability that is not only protected under the American Disabilities Act (ADA) but is also protected in many other countries as well. If any of your allowances for your dyslexic employee affects others in your employ, you may consider allowing for training that helps them better understand what dyslexia is and how it affects workplace performance. With knowledge comes understanding and acceptance, along with a willingness to support and create a positive working environment.

Another option for those who struggle with time management is to arrange tools for them to use, such as an electronic reminder system for appointments and deadlines. Another option is to offer them a time management scheduling software to keep them on point with their necessary tasks for the day. It is important to remember that dyslexia can cause an otherwise productive employee to slow down when it comes to tasks such as reading, writing, filing, etc. They may need to be allotted extra time to finish a task, and you may need to take that into consideration when handing out time-sensitive projects.

As a Friend

As a friend going in, it can be difficult to understand what being dyslexic is like. One of the most basic concepts that can help to understand is that it is hard to focus. Dyslexia can be far more than just having difficulties with reading and writing. Because of the way they process things, dyslexics may have difficulties communicating or communicate in a way that seems weird to you. They also think differently, process things differently, and ultimately see things differently than do the rest of us.

Dyslexics can almost be autistic in nature, not understanding social cues, or what is acceptable for public discussion. It can also be a hit or miss type of thing. Some days they may not seem to have any difficulties at all functioning like everyone else, but they have bad days, just like everyone else. They can be extremely creative and artistic individuals, but you need to remember that they usually have to work harder at everything than everyone else does. This can exhaust them very easily, and they prefer to think in larger, more abstract concepts than to focus on the details that make their brains tired.

One of the best things you can do is talk about how dyslexia affects them and then put yourself in their shoes. Think about how it would make you feel if you saw the world or struggled the same way that they do. Ask yourself how you would like to be treated and do the same for your friend.

Don't just do things for them, watch for signs that they may be struggling or are in need of help, like reading a menu at a restaurant. Try to be discreet. Many people with dyslexia are embarrassed by the fact that they struggle with it. Instead of asking whether they need help, especially if others are around, point out something that you know they enjoy... "Hey, look, they have spicy fries!"

When talking to them about their dyslexia, or if you encounter a problem, later on, ask them if they have any boundaries, they would like you to maintain. Do they want you to help them? Or do they want to work on things themselves when they struggle? Let them know that whatever they decide, you are there for them and will work to help them in whatever way they feel comfortable.

Dyslexia may be a disability, but dyslexics are still high functioning members of our society with incredible insights that we may not be able to either experience or understand. Take the time to realize that they may feel this way about you, too, and work together to achieve greatness!

CONCLUSION

Thank you for making it through to the end of The World of Dyslexia: Understanding how to work with the dyslexic brain., let's hope it was informative and able to provide you with all of the tools you need to achieve your goals whatever they may be.

The next step is to find out the best ways that you can offer help and assistance to the dyslexic in your life so that they have the opportunity to achieve their best and highest successes in life.

Finally, if you found this book useful in any way, a review on Amazon is always appreciated! Thank you!

Printed in Great Britain
by Amazon

69296263R00072